By LADY GREGORY

Drama

Seven Short Plays.

Folk-History Plays. 2 vols.

New Comedies.

The Golden Apple.

The Dragon.

Our Irish Theatre. A Chapter of Autobiography.

The Kiltartan Molière.

The Image and Other Plays.

Three Wonder Plays.

Irish Folk-Lore and Legend

Visions and Beliefs. 2 vols.

Cuchulain of Murithemne.

Gods and Fighting Men.

Saints and Wonders.

Poets and Dreamers.

The Kiltartan Poetry Book.

The Kiltartan History Book.

Hugh Lane's Life and Achievement, with Some Account of the Dublin Galleries.

Augusta Gregory

Our Irish Theatre

A Chapter of Autobiography

By

Isabella Augusta (Persse) Gregory

Lady Gregory 1859-

Illustrated

G. P. Putnam's Sons
London and New York

The Knickerbocker Press
New York

Made in the United States of America

CONTENTS

APPENDICES

ILLUSTRATIONS

Our Irish Theatre

CHAPTER I

THE THEATRE IN THE MAKING

To Richard Gregory.—Little Grandson: When I go into the garden in the morning to find you a nectarine or tell you the names of flowers, Catalpa, Love-lies-bleeding, Balsam, Phlox, you ask me why I cannot stay but must go back to the house, and when I say it is to write letters, you ask, "What for?" And when winter comes, you will ask me why I must go away over the sea instead of waiting for your Christmas stocking and your tree.

The other day I was sitting outside the door, where the sweet-peas grow, with an old man, and when you came and called me he got up to go away, and as he wished me good-bye, he said: "They were telling me you are going to America, and says I, 'Whatever the Lady does, I am certain she is doing nothing but what she thinks to be right.' And that the Lord may keep you safe and protect you from the power of your enemy."

Some day when I am not here to answer, you will maybe ask, "What were they for, the writing, the journeys, and why did she have an enemy?" So I will put down the story now, that you may know all about it bye and bye.

Fourteen or fifteen years ago I still wrote from time to time in a diary I used to keep till the sand in the hour-glass on my table began to run so fast that I had to lay by the book as well as embroidery, and archæology, and drying lavender, and visits to the houses of friends.

I was in London in the beginning of 1898, and I find written, "Yeats and Sir Alfred Lyall to tea, Yeats stayed on. He is very full of playwriting. . . . He with the aid of Miss Florence Farr, an actress who thinks more of a romantic than of a paying play, is very keen about taking or building a little theatre somewhere in the suburbs to produce romantic drama, his own plays, Edward Martyn's, one of Bridges', and he is trying to stir up Standish O'Grady and Fiona Macleod to write some. He believes there will be a reaction after the realism of Ibsen, and romance will have its turn. He has put a 'great deal of himself' into his own play *The Shadowy Waters* and rather startled me by saying about half his characters have eagles' faces."

Later in the year I was staying for a few days with old Count de Basterot, at Duras, that is beyond Kinvara and beside the sea. He had been my husband's warm friend, and always in the summer time we used to go and spend at least one long day with him,—we two at first, and then later I went with my son and the boy and girl friends of his childhood. They liked to go out in a hooker and see the seals showing their heads, or to paddle delicately among the jellyfish on the beach. It was a pleasant place to pass an idle day. The garden was full of flowers. Lavender and carnations grew best, and there were roses also and apple trees, and many plums ripened on the walls. This seemed strange, because outside the sheltered garden there were only stone-strewn fields and rocks and bare rock-built hills in sight, and the bay of Galway, over which fierce storms blow from the Atlantic. The Count remembered when on Garlic Sunday men used to ride races, naked, on unsaddled horses out into the sea; but that wild custom had long been done away with by decree of the priests. Later still, when Harrow and Oxford took my son away and I had long spaces of time alone, I would sometimes go to Duras to spend a few days.

I always liked to talk and to listen to the Count. He could tell me about French books and French and Italian history and politics, for he lived but for the summer months in Ireland and for the rest of the year in Paris or in Rome. Mr. Arthur Symons has written of him and his talks of race,—to which he attributed all good or bad habits and politics—as they took long drives on the Campagna. M. Paul Bourget came more than once to stay in this Burren district, upon which he bestowed a witty name, "Le Royaume de Pierre." It was to M. Bourget that on his way to the modest little house and small estate, the Count's old steward and servant introduced the Atlantic, when on the road from the railway station at Gort its waters first come in sight: *Voila la mer qui baigne l'Amérique et les terres de Monsieur le Comte.* For he—the steward—had been taken by his master on visits to kinsmen in France and Italy—their names are recorded in that sad, pompous, black-bordered document I received one day signed by those who have *l'honneur de vous faire part de la perte douloureuse qu'ils viennent d'éprouver en la personne de Florimond Alfred Jacques, Comte de Basterot, Chevalier de l'ordre du Saint Sépulcre, leur cousin germain et cousin* [who died at Duras (Irlande) September 15, 1904]; *la Marquise de la Tour Maubourg, le Vicomte et la Vicomtesse de Bussy, la Baronne d'Acker de Montgaston, le Marquis et la Marquise de Courcival, le Comte et la Comtesse Gromis de Trana, la Comtesse Irène d' Entreves*, and so on, and so on. I do not know whether the bearers of these high-sounding names keep him in their memory—it may well be that they do, for he was a friend not easily forgotten—but I know there is many a prayer still said on the roads between Kinvara and Burren and Curranroe and Ballinderreen for him who "never was without a bag of money to give in charity, and always had a heart for the poor."

On one of those days at Duras in 1898, Mr. Edward Martyn, my neighbour, came to see the Count, bringing with him Mr. Yeats, whom I did not then know very well, though I cared for his work very much and had already, through his directions, been gathering folk-lore. They had lunch with us, but it was a wet day, and we could not go out. After a while I thought the Count wanted to talk to Mr. Martyn alone; so I took Mr. Yeats to the office where the steward used to come to talk,—less about business I think than of the Land War or the state of the country, or the last year's deaths and marriages from Kinvara to the headland of Aughanish. We sat there through that wet afternoon, and though I had never been at all interested in theatres, our talk turned on plays. Mr. Martyn had written two, *The Heather Field* and *Maeve*. They had been offered to London managers, and now he thought of trying to have them produced in Germany where there seemed to be more room for new drama than in England. I said it was a pity we had no Irish theatre where such plays could be given. Mr. Yeats said that had always been a dream of his, but he had of late thought it an impossible one, for it could not at first pay its way, and there was no money to be found for such a thing in Ireland.

We went on talking about it, and things seemed

to grow possible as we talked, and before the end of the afternoon we had made our plan. We said we would collect money, or rather ask to have a certain sum of money guaranteed. We would then take a Dublin theatre and give a performance of Mr. Martyn's *Heather Field* and one of Mr. Yeats's own plays, *The Countess Cathleen.* I offered the first guarantee of £25.

A few days after that I was back at Coole, and Mr. Yeats came over from Mr. Martyn's home, Tillyra, and we wrote a formal letter to send out. We neither of us write a very clear hand, but a friend had just given me a Remington typewriter and I was learning to use it, and I wrote out the letter with its help. That typewriter has done a great deal of work since that day, making it easy for the printers to read my plays and translations, and Mr. Yeats's plays and essays, and sometimes his poems. I have used it also for the many, many hundreds of letters that have had to be written about theatre business in each of these last fifteen years. It has gone with me very often up and down to Dublin and back again, and it went with me even to America last year that I might write my letters home. And while I am writing the leaves are falling, and since I have written those last words on its keys, she who had given it to me has gone. She gave me also the great gift of her friendship through more than half my lifetime, Enid, Lady Layard, Ambassadress at Constantinople and Madrid, helper of the miserable and the wounded in the Turkish-Russian war; helper of the sick in the hospital she founded at Venice, friend and hostess and guest of queens in England and Germany and Rome. She was her husband's good helpmate while he lived—is not the Cyprus treaty set down in that clear handwriting I shall never see coming here again? And widowed, she kept his name in honour, living after him for fifteen years, and herself leaving a noble memory in all places where she had stayed, and in Venice where her home was and where she died.

Our statement—it seems now a little pompous—began:

"We propose to have performed in Dublin, in the spring of every year certain Celtic and Irish plays, which whatever be their degree of excellence will be written with a high ambition, and so to build up a Celtic and Irish school of dramatic literature. We hope to find in Ireland an uncorrupted and imaginative audience trained to listen by its passion for oratory, and believe that our desire to bring upon the stage the deeper thoughts and emotions of Ireland will ensure for us a tolerant welcome, and that freedom to experiment which is not found in theatres of England, and without which no new movement in art or literature can succeed. We will show that Ireland is not the home of buffoonery and of easy sentiment, as it has been represented, but the home of an ancient idealism. We are confident of the support of all Irish people, who are weary of misrepresentation, in carrying out a work that is outside all the political questions that divide us."

I think the word "Celtic" was put in for the sake of Fiona Macleod whose plays however we never acted, though we used to amuse ourselves by thinking of the call for "author" that might follow one, and the possible appearance of William Sharp in place of the beautiful woman he had given her out to be, for even then we had little doubt they were one and the same person. I myself never quite understood the meaning of the "Celtic Movement," which we were said to belong to.

When I was asked about it, I used to say it was a movement meant to persuade the Scotch to begin buying our books, while we continued not to buy theirs.

We asked for a guarantee fund of £300 to make the experiment, which we hoped to carry on during three years. The first person I wrote to was the old poet, Aubrey de Vere. He answered very kindly, saying, "Whatever develops the genius of Ireland, must in the most effectual way benefit her; and in Ireland's genius I have long been a strong believer. Circumstances of very various sorts have hitherto tended much to retard the development of that genius; but it cannot fail to make itself recognised before very long, and Ireland will have cause for gratitude to all those who have hastened the coming of that day."

I am glad we had this letter, carrying as it were the blessing of the generation passing away to that which was taking its place. He was the first poet I had ever met and spoken with; he had come in my girlhood to a neighbour's house. He was so gentle, so fragile, he seemed to have been wafted in by that "wind from the plains of Athenry" of which he wrote in one of his most charming little poems. He was of the Lake School, and talked of Wordsworth, and I think it was as a sort of courtesy or deference to him that I determined to finish reading *The Excursion*, which though a reader of poetry it had failed me, as we say, to get through. At last one morning I climbed up to a wide wood, Grobawn, on one of the hillsides of Slieve Echtge, determined not to come down again until I had honestly read every line. I think I saw the sun set behind the far-off Connemara hills before I came home, exhausted but triumphant! I have a charming picture of Aubrey de Vere in my mind as I last saw him, at a garden party in London. He was walking about, having on his arm, in the old-world style, the beautiful Lady Somers, lovely to the last as in Thackeray's day, and as I had heard of her from many of that time, and as she had been painted by Watts.

Some gave us their promise with enthusiasm but some from good will only, without much faith that an Irish Theatre would ever come to success. One friend, a writer of historical romance, wrote: "October 15th. I enclose a cheque for £1, but confess it is more as a proof of regard for *you* than of belief in the drama, for I cannot with the best wish in the world to do so, feel hopeful on that subject. My experience has been that any attempt at treating Irish history is a fatal handicap, not to say absolute *bar*, to anything in the shape of popularity, and I cannot see how any drama can flourish which is not to some degree supported by the public, as it is even more dependent on it than literature is. There *are* popular Irish dramatists, of course, and *very* popular ones, but then unhappily they did not treat of Irish subjects, and *The School for Scandal* and *She Stoops to Conquer* would hardly come under your category. You will think me very discouraging, but I cannot help it, and I am also afraid that putting plays experimentally on the boards is a very costly entertainment. Where will they be acted in the first instance? And has any stage manager undertaken to produce them? Forgive my tiresomeness; it does not come from want of sympathy, only from a little want of hope, the result of experience."

"October 19th. I seize the opportunity of writing again as I am afraid you will have thought I wrote such an unsympathetic letter. It is not, believe me, that I would not give anything to see Irish literature and Irish drama taking a good place, as it ought to do, and several of the authors you name I admire extremely. It is only from the practical and *paying* point of view that I feel it to be rather rash. Plays cost more, I take it, to produce than novels, and one would feel rather rash if one brought out a novel at one's own risk."

I think the only actual refusals I had were from three members of the Upper House. I may give their words as types of the discouragement we have often met with from friends: "I need not, I am sure, tell you how gladly I would take part in anything for the honour of Old Ireland and especially anything of the kind in which you feel an interest; but I must tell you frankly that I do not much believe in the movement about which you have written to me. I have no sympathy, you will be horrified to hear, with the 'London Independent Theatre,' and I am sure that if Ibsen and Co. could know what is in my mind, they would regard me as a 'Philistine' of the coarsest class! Alas! so far from wishing to see the Irish characters of Charles Lever supplanted by more refined types, they have always been the delight of my heart, and there is no author in whose healthy, rollicking company, even nowadays, I spend a spare hour with more thorough enjoyment. I am very sorry that I cannot agree with you in these matters, and I am irreclaimable; but all the same I remain with many pleasant remembrances and good wishes for you and yours, Yours very truly——"

Another, the late Lord Ashbourne, wrote: "I know too little of the matter or the practicability of the idea to be able to give my name to your list, but I shall watch the experiment with interest and be glad to attend. The idea is novel and curious, and how far it is capable of realisation I am not at all in a position to judge. Some of the names you mention are well known in literature but not as dramatists or playwriters, and therefore the public will be one to be worked up by enthusiasm and love of country. The existing class of actors will not, of course, be available, and the existing playgoers are satisfied with their present attractions. Whether 'houses' can be got to attend the new plays, founded on new ideas and played by new actors, no one can foretell."

One, who curiously has since then become an almost too zealous supporter of our theatre, says: "I fear I am not sanguine about the success in a pecuniary way of a 'Celtic Theatre,' nor am I familiar with the works, dramatic or otherwise, of Mr. Yeats or of Mr. Martyn. Therefore, at the risk of branding myself in your estimation as a hopeless Saxon and Philistine, I regret I cannot see my way to giving my name to the enterprise or joining in the guarantee." On the other hand, Professor Mahaffy says, rather unexpectedly, writing from Trinity College: "I am ready to risk £5 for your scheme and hope they may yet play their drama in Irish. It will be as intelligible to the nation as Italian, which we so often hear upon our stage."

And many joined who had seemed too far apart to join in any scheme. Mr. William Harpole Lecky sent a promise of £5 instead of the £1 I had asked. Lord Dufferin, Viceroy of India and Canada, Ambassador at Paris, Constantinople, St. Petersburg, and Rome, not only promised but sent his guarantee in advance. I returned it later, for the sums guaranteed were never called for, Mr. Martyn very generously making up all loss. Miss Jane Barlow, Miss Emily Lawless, the Lord Chancellor of Ireland ("Peter the Packer" as he was called by Nationalists), John O'Leary, Mr. T. M. Healy, Lord and Lady Ardilaun, the Duchess of St. Albans, Doctor Douglas Hyde, the Rt. Hon. Horace Plunkett, Mr. John Dillon, M. P., all joined. Mr. John Redmond supported us, and afterwards wrote me a letter of commendation with leave to use it. Mr. William O'Brien was another supporter. I did not know him personally but I remember one day long ago going to tea at the Speaker's house, after I had heard him in a debate, and saying I thought him the most stirring speaker of all the Irish party; and I was amused when my gentle and dignified hostess, Mrs. Peel, said, "I quite agree with you. When I hear William O'Brien make a speech, I feel that if I were an Irishwoman, I should like to go and break windows."

Then Mr. Yeats and Mr. Martyn went to Dublin to make preparations, but the way was unexpectedly blocked by the impossibility of getting a theatre. The only Dublin theatres, the Gaiety, the Royal, and the Queen's, were engaged far ahead, and in any case we could not have given them their price. Then we thought of taking a hall or a concert room, but there again we met with disappointment. We found there was an old Act in existence, passed just before the Union, putting a fine of £300 upon any one who should give a performance for money in any unlicensed building. As the three large theatres were the only buildings licensed, a claim for a special license would have to be argued by lawyers, charging lawyers' fees, before the Privy Council. We found that even amateurs who acted for charities were forced to take one of the licensed theatres, so leaving but little profit for the charity. There were suggestions made of forming a society like the Stage Society in London, to give performances to its members only, but this would not have been a fit beginning for the National Theatre of our dreams. I wrote in a letter at that time: "I am all for having the Act repealed or a Bill brought in, empowering the Municipality to license halls when desirable." And although this was looked on as a counsel of perfection, it was actually done within the year. I wrote to Mr. Lecky for advice and help, and he told me there was a Bill actually going through the House of Commons, the Local Government (Ireland) Bill, in which he thought it possible a Clause might be inserted that would meet our case. Mr. John Redmond and Mr. Dillon promised their help; so did Mr. T. M. Healy, who wrote to Mr. Yeats: "I am acquainted with the state of the law in Dublin which I should gladly assist to alter as proposed. Whether the Government are equally well disposed may be doubted, as the subject is a little outside their Bill, and no adequate time exists for discussing it and many other important questions. They will come up about midnight or later and will be yawned out of hearing by our masters."

A Clause was drawn up by a Nationalist member, Mr. Clancy, but in July, 1898, Mr. Lecky writes from the House of Commons: "I have not been forgetting the Celtic Theatre and I think the enclosed Clause, which the Government have brought forward, will practically meet its requirements. The Attorney-General objected to Mr. Clancy's Clause as too wide and as interfering with existing patent rights, but promised a Clause authorising amateur acting. I wrote to him, however, stating the Celtic case, and urging that writers should be able, like those who got up the Ibsen plays in London, to get regular actors to play for them, and I think this Clause will allow it. . . . After Clause 59 insert the following Clause: (1) Notwithstanding anything in the Act of Parliament of Ireland of the twenty-sixth year of King George the Third, Chapter fifty-seven, intituled an Act for regulating the stage in the city and county of Dublin, the Lord Lieutenant may on the application of the council for the county of Dublin or the county borough of Dublin grant an occasional license for the performance of any stage play or other dramatic entertainment in any theatre, room, or building where the profits arising therefrom are to be applied for charitable purpose or in aid of the funds of any society instituted for the purpose of science, literature, or the fine arts exclusively. (2) The license may contain such conditions and regulations as appear fit to the Lord Lieutenant, and may be revoked by him."

This Clause was passed but we are independent now of it,—the Abbey Theatre holds its own Patent. But the many amateur societies which play so often here and there in Dublin may well call for a blessing sometimes on the names of those by whom their charter was won.

We announced our first performance for May 8, 1899, nearly a year after that talk on the Galway coast, at the Ancient Concert Rooms. Mr. Yeats' *Countess Cathleen* and Mr. Martyn's *Heather Field* were the plays chosen, as we had planned at the first. Mr. George Moore gave excellent help in finding actors, and the plays were rehearsed in London. But then something unexpected happened. A writer who had a political quarrel with Mr. Yeats sent out a pamphlet in which he attacked *The Countess Cathleen*, on the ground of religious unorthodoxy. The plot of the play, taken from an old legend, is this: during a famine in Ireland some starving country people, having been tempted by demons dressed as merchants to sell their souls for money that their bodies may be saved from perishing, the Countess Cathleen sells her own soul to redeem theirs, and dies. The accusation made was that it was a libel on the people of Ireland to say they could under any circumstances consent to sell their souls and that it was a libel on the demons that they counted the soul of a countess of more worth than those of the poor. At Cathleen's death the play tells us, "God looks on the intention, not the deed," and so she is forgiven at the last and taken into Heaven; and this it was said is against the teaching of the Church.

Mr. Martyn is an orthodox Catholic, and to quiet his mind, the play was submitted to two good Churchmen. Neither found heresy enough in it to call for its withdrawal. One of them, the Rev. Dr. Barry, the author of *The New Antigone*, wrote:

"BRIDGE HOUSE, WALLINGFORD,
"March 26, 1899."

"DEAR MR. YEATS,

"I read your *Countess Cathleen* as soon as possible after seeing you. It is beautiful and touching. I hope you will not be kept back from giving it by foolish talk. Obviously, from the literal point of view theologians, Catholic or other, would object that no one is free to sell his soul in order to buy bread even for the starving. But St. Paul says, 'I wish to be anathema for my brethren'; which is another way of expressing what you have put into a story. I would give the play first and explanations afterwards.

"Sometime perhaps you will come and spend a night here and I shall be charmed. But don't take a superfluous journey now. It is an awkward place to get at. I could only tell you, as I am doing, that if people will not read or look at a play of this kind in the spirit which dictated it, no change you might make would satisfy them. You have given us what is really an Auto, in the manner of Calderon, with the old Irish folk-lore as a perceptive; and to measure it by the iron rule of experts and schoolmen would be most unfair to it. Some one else will say that you have learned from the Jesuits to make the end justify the means—and much that man will know of you or the Jesuits. With many kind wishes for your success, and fraternal greetings in the name of Ireland,

"Ever yours,

"William Barry."

So our preparations went on. Mr. Yeats wrote a little time before the first performance: "Everybody tells me we are going to have good audiences. My play, too, in acting goes wonderfully well. The actors are all pretty sound.

The first Demon is a little over-violent and restless but he will improve. Lionel Johnson has done a prologue which I enclose."

That prologue, written by so Catholic and orthodox a poet, was spoken before the plays at the Ancient Concert Rooms on May 8, 1899:

The May fire once on every dreaming hill
All the fair land with burning bloom would fill;
All the fair land, at visionary night,
Gave loving glory to the Lord of Light.
Have we no leaping flames of Beltaine praise
To kindle in the joyous ancient ways;
No fire of song, of vision, of white dream,
Fit for the Master of the Heavenly Gleam;
For him who first made Ireland move in chime,
Musical from the misty dawn of time?

Ah, yes; for sacrifice this night we bring
The passion of a lost soul's triumphing;
All rich with faery airs that, wandering long,
Uncaught, here gather into Irish song;
Sweet as the old remembering winds that wail,
From hill to hill of gracious Inisfail;
Sad as the unforgetting winds that pass
Over her children in her holy grass
At home, and sleeping well upon her breast,
Where snowy Deirdre and her sorrows rest.

Come, then, and keep with us an Irish feast,
Wherein the Lord of Light and Song is priest;
Now, at this opening of the gentle May,
Watch warring passions at their storm and play;
Wrought with the flaming ecstasy of art,
Sprung from the dreaming of an Irish heart.

But alas! His call to "watch warring passions at their storm and play," was no vain one. The pamphlet, *Souls for Gold*, had been sent about, and sentences spoken by the demons in the play and given detached from it were quoted as Mr. Yeats' own unholy beliefs. A Cardinal who confessed he had read none of the play outside these sentences condemned it. Young men from the Catholic University were roused to come and make a protest against this "insult to their faith." There was hooting and booing in the gallery. In the end the gallery was lined with police, for an attack on the actors was feared. They, being English and ignorant of Ireland, found it hard to understand the excitement, but they went through their parts very well. There was enthusiasm for both plays, and after the first night London critics were sent over, Mr. Max Beerbohm among them, and gave a good report. Yet it was a stormy beginning for our enterprise, and a rough reception for a poetic play. The only moment, I think, at which I saw Mr. Yeats really angry was at the last performance. I was sitting next him, and the play had reached the point where the stage direction says, "The Second Merchant goes out through the door and returns with the hen strangled. He flings it on the floor." The merchant came in indeed, but without the strangled hen. Mr. Yeats got up, filled with suspicions that it also might have been objected to on some unknown ground, and went round to the back of the stage. But he was given a simple explanation. The chief Demon said he had been given charge of the hen, and had hung it out of a window every night, "And this morning," he said, "when I pulled up the string, there was nothing on it at all."

But that battle was not a very real one. We have put on *Countess Cathleen* a good many times of late with no one speaking against it at all. And some of those young men who hissed it then are our good supporters now.

The next year English actors were again brought over to play, this time in the Gaiety Theatre. A little play by Miss Milligan, *The Last Feast of the Fianna* was given, and Mr. Martyn's *Maeve*, and on alternate nights *The Bending of the Bough*, founded by Mr. George Moore on Mr. Martyn's *Tale of a Town*. They were produced on the evening of February 20, 1900. "On the evening before the production," I wrote, "Mr. Yeats gave a little address on the play, *Maeve*, in which he said there is a wonderful literary invention, that of Peg Inerny, the old woman in rags in the daytime, but living another and second life, a queen in the ideal world, a symbol of Ireland. The financial question touched in *The Bending of the Bough* was chosen, because on it all parties are united, but it means really the cause nearest to each of our hearts. The materialism of England and its vulgarity are surging up about us. It is not Shakespeare England sends us, but musical farces, not Keats and Shelley, but *Titbits*. A mystic friend of his had a dream in which he saw a candle whose flame was in danger of being extinguished by a rolling sea. The waves sometimes seemed to go over it and quench it, and he knew it to be his own soul and that if it was quenched, he would have lost his soul. And now our ideal life is in danger from the sea of commonness about us."

The Bending of the Bough was the first play dealing with a vital Irish question that had appeared in Ireland. There was a great deal of excitement over it. My diary says: "M. is in great enthusiasm over it, says it will cause a revolution. H. says no young man can see that play and leave the house as he came into it. . . . The Gaelic League in great force sang *Fainne Geal an Lae* between the acts, and *The Wearing of the Green* in Irish! And when 'author' could not appear, there were cries of 'An Craoibhin,' and cheers were given for Hyde. The actors say they never played to so appreciative an audience, but were a little puzzled at the applause, not understanding the political allusions. The play hits so impartially all round that no one is really offended, certainly not the Nationalists and we have not heard that Unionists are either. Curiously, *Maeve*, which we did n't think a Nationalist play at all, has turned out to be one, the audience understanding and applauding the allegory. There is such applause at 'I am only an old woman, but I tell you that Erin will never be subdued' that

Lady ——, who was at a performance, reported to the Castle that they had better boycott it, which they have done. G. M. is, I think, a little puzzled by his present political position, but I tell him and E. Martyn we are not working for Home Rule; we are preparing for it."

In our third year, 1901, Mr. F. R. Benson took our burden on his shoulders and gave a fine performance of *Diarmuid and Grania*, an heroic play by Mr. George Moore and Mr. Yeats. I wrote: "I am so glad to hear of Benson's appreciation. Anyhow, he can hardly be supposed to be on the side of incendiarism; he is so very respectable. Trinity College won't know whether to go or to stay away." Mr. Yeats wrote: "Yesterday we were rehearsing at the Gaiety. The kid Benson is to carry in his arms was wandering in and out among the stage properties. I was saying to myself, 'Here are we, a lot of intelligent people who might have been doing some sort of decent work that leaves the soul free; yet here we are, going through all sorts of trouble and annoyance for a mob that knows neither literature nor art. I might have been away, away in the country, in Italy perhaps, writing poems for my equals and my betters. That kid is the only sensible creature on the stage. He knows his business and keeps to it.' At that very moment one of the actors called out, 'Look at the kid, eating the property ivy!' "

This time also we produced *Casad-an-Sugan*, (*The Twisting of the Rope*) by the founder of the Gaelic League, Dr. Douglas Hyde. He himself acted the chief part in it and even to those who had no Irish, the performance was a delight, it was played with so much gaiety, ease, and charm. It was the first time a play written in Irish had ever been see in a Dublin theatre.

Our three years' experiment had ended, and we hesitated what to do next. But a breaking and rebuilding is often for the best, and so it was now. We had up to this time, as I have said, played only once a year, and had engaged actors from London, some of them Irish certainly, but all London-trained. The time had come to play oftener and to train actors of our own. For Mr. Yeats had never ceased attacking the methods of the ordinary theatre, in gesture, in staging, and in the speaking of verse. It happened there were two brothers living in Dublin, William and Frank Fay, who had been in the habit of playing little farces in coffee palaces and such like in their spare time. William had a genius for comedy, Frank's ambitions were for the production of verse. They, or one of them, had thought of looking for work in America, but had seen our performances, and thought something might be done in the way of creating a school of acting in Ireland. They came to us at this time and talked matters over. They had work to do in the daytime and could only rehearse at night. The result was that Mr. Yeats gave his *Kathleen ni Houlihan* to be produced by Mr. Fay at the same time as a play by Mr. George Russell (A.E.), in St. Theresa's Hall, Clarendon Street. I had written to Mr. Yeats: "If all breaks up, we must try and settle something with Fay, possibly a week of the little plays he has been doing through the spring. I have a sketch in my head that might do for Hyde to work on. I will see if it is too slight when I have noted it down, and if not, will send it to you."

Early, in 1902, Mr. Russell wrote to me: "I have finished *Deirdre* at last. Heaven be praised! in the intervals of railway journeys, and the Fays are going to do their best with it. I hope I shall not suffer too much in the process, but I prefer them to English actors as they are in love with their story." A little hall in Camden Street was hired for rehearsal, Mr. Russell writing in the same year: "I will hand cheque to Fay. I know it will be a great assistance to them as the little hall will require alterations and fittings and as none of the Company are in possession of more than artisan's wages. They have elected W. B. Y. as president of the Irish National Dramatic Society, and A. E. as vice-president, and we are the gilding at the prow of the vessel. They have begun work already and are reading and rehearsing drama for the autumn."

Mr. Fay was very hopeful and full of courage. He wrote in December, 1902: "I have received your letter and parcel. I am not doing this show on a large scale as I am leaving *The Hour-glass* off till the middle of January. . . . I am just giving a show of *The Pot of Broth*, *The Foundations*, and *Elis and the Beggarman*, and I 'm not making a fuss about it, as I want to try how many people the hall will hold, and what prices suit best, so it is more or less an experimental show and then, about the middle of January, I will do the first real show with *The Hour-glass* as principal feature. The hall took a great deal of work to get right, and as we had to do all the work ourselves, we had very little time to rehearse." And he says later: "I received your kind note, also enclosures, for which we are very much obliged. We are indeed getting into very flourishing conditions, and if things only continue in the present state, I have no doubt we shall be able to show a fairly good balance at the end of the year. I have all but concluded an arrangement with a branch of the Gaelic League to take our hall for three nights a week, and that will leave us under very small rental if it comes off. About the performance and how it worked out. I spent twenty-five shillings on printing, etc., and we took altogether about four pounds fifteen shillings, so I see no reason to complain financially. But I find the stage very small, and the want of dressing-rooms makes it very difficult to manage about the scenery, as all your actors have to stand against the walls while it is being changed. I think, however, we can struggle through if we don't attempt very large pieces. The hall was rather cold, but I think I can manage a stove and get over that."

That show of *The Hour-glass* went well, and in that year—1903—two of Mr. Yeats's verse plays were produced, *The King's Threshold* and *Shadowy Waters*. In that year also, new names came in, my own with *Twenty-five*, Mr. Padraic Colum's with *Broken Soil*, and that of J. M. Synge with *The Shadow of the Glen*. I wrote to Mr. Yeats, who was then in America: "After *Shadow of the Glen* your sisters and Synge came in and had some supper with me. Your sister had asked one of her work girls how she liked Synge's comedy, and she said, 'Oh, very well. I had been thinking of writing a story on that subject myself.' They asked quite a little girl if she thought the girl in Colum's play ought to have stayed with her lover or gone with her father. 'She was right to go with her father.' 'Why?' 'Because her young man had such a big beard.' 'But he might have cut it off.' 'That would be no good. He was so dark he would look blue if he did that.' Saturday night brought a larger audience and all went well. The few I knew, Harvey, etc., were quite astonished at the beauty of *Shadowy Waters*, and some giggling young men behind were hushed almost at once, and I heard them saying afterwards how beautiful it was. I should like to hear it once a week through the whole year. The only vexing part was Aibric's helmet, which has immense horns. A black shadow of these was thrown down, and when Aibric moved, one got the impression there was a he-goat going to butt at him over the side of the ship." And again from Coole: "Synge wrote asking me if I could provide four red petticoats, Aran men's caps, a spinning-wheel, and some Connacht person in Dublin who will teach the players to keen. The last item is the most difficult. All the actors want pampooties (the cowskin shoes worn by the Aran people), though I warned them the smell is rather overpowering. Tell Mr. Quinn what a great comfort his money is for such things as these, upon which the company might think they ought not to spend their little capital, and Synge would have been unhappy without." Through the nuns at Gort I heard of a spinning-wheel in a cottage some way off, which, though it had been in her family over a hundred years, the owner wanted to sell. A cart was sent for this, and we have had it in the theatre ever since. As to the keening I found a Galway woman near Dublin who promised to teach the actors. But when they arrived at her house, she found herself unable to raise the keen in her living room. They had all to go upstairs, and the secretary of the company had to lie under a sheet as the corpse. The lessons were very successful, and at the first performance in London of *Riders to the Sea*, the pit went away keening down the street.

Mr. Yeats said of Mr. Fay and his little company, "They did what amateurs seldom do, worked desperately." This was the beginning of a native school of acting, an Irish dramatic company.

I remember, in 1897, hearing Mr. Bernard Shaw make a speech before the Irish Literary Society in London, following a lecture on "Irish Actors of the Nineteenth Century." He very wittily extinguished the lecturer, who, he said, truly enough had enumerated the best actors and actresses and then had gone on to say they were not Irish. "As to what an Irishman is," he said, "is a complex question, for wherever he may have been born, if he has been brought up in Ireland, that is quite sufficient to make him an Irishman. It is a mistake to think an Irishman has not common sense. It is the Englishman who is devoid of common sense or at least has so small a portion of it that he can only apply it to the work immediately before him. That is why he is obliged to fill the rest of his horizon with the humbugs and hypocrisy that fill so large a part of English life. The Irishman has a better grasp of facts and sees them more clearly; only he fails in putting them into practice, and has a great objection to doing anything that will lead to any practical result. It is a mistake to think the Irishman has feeling; he has not; but the Englishman is full of feeling. What the Irishman has is imagination; he can imagine himself in the situation of others." Then as if afraid of making the Irish members of his audience too well pleased with themselves, he gave his summing up: "But the Irish language is an effete language and the nation is effete, and as to saying there are good Irish actors, there are not, and there won't be until the conditions in Ireland are favourable for the production of drama, and when that day comes, I hope I may be dead."

I am glad we have shown Mr. Shaw that he can be in the wrong, and I am glad he is not dead, for he has been a good friend to us. But our players have proved that even the wise may be deceived. They have won much praise for themselves and have raised the dignity of Ireland, and I for one owe them very grateful thanks for the way they have made the characters in my comedies laugh and live.

In May, 1903, the Irish National Theatre Society went for the first time to London. It was hard for the actors to get away. They had their own work to do. But they asked their employers a for whole Saturday holiday. They left Dublin on Friday night, arrived in London on the Saturday morning, played in the afternoon, and again in the evening at the Queen's Gate Hall, and were back at work in Dublin on Monday morning. The plays taken were: Mr. Fred Ryan's *Laying the Foundations*, Mr. Yeats's *Hour-glass*, *Pot of Broth*, and *Kathleen in Houlihan*, and my own *Twenty-five*. I was not able to go but Mr. Yeats wrote to me: "London, May 4, '03. The plays were a great success. I never saw a more enthusiastic audience. I send you some papers, all that I have found notices in. When I remember the notices I have seen of literary adventures on the stage, I think them better than we could have hoped. . . . I have noticed that the young men, the men of my own generation or younger, are the people who like us. It was a very distinguished audience. Blunt was there, but went after your play as he is just recovering from influenza and seems to be really ill. I thought your play went very well. Fay was charming as Christy. The game of cards is still the weak place, but with all defects, the little play has a real charm. If we could amend the cards it would be a strong play too. Lady Aberdeen, Henry James, Michael Field—who has sent me an enthusiastic letter about the acting—Mrs. Wyndham—the Chief Secretary's mother—Lord Monteagle, Mrs. Thackeray Ritchie, and I don't know how many other notables were there, and all I think were moved. The evening audience was the more Irish and *Kathleen* and *The Pot of Broth* got a great reception. *The Foundations* went well, indeed everything went well."

This was but the first of several London visits, and the good audience and good notices were a great encouragement. And this visit led also to the generous help given us by Miss Horniman. She took what had been the old Mechanics' Institute in Abbey Street, Dublin, adding to it a part of the site of the old Morgue, and by rebuilding and reconstructing turned it into what has since been known as the Abbey Theatre, giving us the free use of it together with an annual subsidy for a term of years.

Miss Horniman did all this, as she says in a former letter to Mr. Yeats, because of her "great sympathy with the artistic and dramatic aims of the Irish National Theatre Company as publicly explained by you on various occasions." She also states in that letter: "I can only afford to make a very little theatre, and it must be quite simple. You all must do the rest to make a powerful and prosperous theatre with a high artistic ideal." We have kept through many attacks and misunderstandings the high artistic ideal we set out with. Our prosperity enabled us to take over the Abbey Theatre two years ago when our Patent and subsidy came to an end. I feel sure Miss Horniman is well pleased that we have been able to show our gratitude by thus proving ourselves worthy of her great and generous gift.

But in Dublin a new theatre cannot be opened except under a Patent from the Crown. This costs money even when not opposed, and if it is opposed, the question has to be argued by counsel, and witnesses have to be called in and examined as if some dangerous conspiracy were being plotted. When our Patent was applied for, the other theatres took fright and believed we might interfere with their gains, and they opposed our application, and there was delay after delay. But at last the enquiry was held before the Privy Council, and Mr. Yeats wrote on its eve: "3d August, 1904. The really important things first. This day is so hot that I have been filled with alarm lest the lake may begin to fall again and the boat be stranded high up on the bank and I be unable to try my new bait. I brought the boat up to a very shallow place the day I left. I have been running about all over the place collecting witnesses and have now quite a number. I will wire to-morrow if there is anything definite about decision. In any case I will write full particulars."

"August 4th. Final decision is postponed until Monday but the battle is won to all intents and purposes. There appears to be no difficulty about our getting a Patent for the plays of the Society. I sent you a paper with the report of

The Abbey Theatre, Dublin

From a photograph by Keogh Bros., Ireland

proceedings, —— and ——, did well for us; but I must say I was rather amused at their anxiety to show that they supported us not out of love for the arts but because of our use as anti-emigration agents and the like. I think I was a bad witness. Counsel did not examine me but asked me to make a statement. The result was, having expected questions and feeling myself left to wander through an immense subject, I said very little. I was disappointed at being hardly cross-examined at all. By that time I had got excited and was thirsting for everybody's blood. One barrister in cross-examining T. P. Gill, who came after me, tried to prove that Ibsen and Maeterlinck were immoral writers. He asked was it not true that a play by Maeterlinck called *The Intruder* had raised an immense outcry in London because of its immorality. Quite involuntarily I cried out, 'My God!' and Edward Martyn burst into a loud fit of laughter. I suppose he must have meant *Monna Vanna*. He also asked if the Irish National Theatre Society had not produced a play which was an attack on marriage. Somebody asked him what was the name of the play. He said it did n't matter and dropped the subject. He had evidently heard some vague rumour about *The Shadow of the Glen*. I forgot to say that William Fay gave his evidence very well, as one would expect. He had the worst task of us all, for O'Shaughnessy, a brow-beating cross-examiner of the usual kind, fastened on to him. Fay, however, had his answer for everything."

The Patent was granted to me, "Dame Augusta Gregory," as Patentee, and in it I was amongst other things "Enjoined and commanded to gather, entertain, govern, privilege, and keep such and so many players," and not to put on the stage any "exhibition of wild beasts or dangerous performances or to allow women or children to be hung from the flies or fixed in positions from which they cannot release themselves." "It being our Royal will and pleasure that for the future our said theatre may be instrumental to the promotion of virtue and instruction of human life."

The building was not ready for us until the end of the year. Mr. Yeats wrote in August: "I have just been down to see the work on the Abbey Theatre. It is all going very quickly and the company should be able to rehearse there in a month. The other day, while digging up some old rubbish in the Morgue, which is being used for dressing-rooms, they found human bones. The workmen thought they had lit on a murder, but the caretaker said, 'Oh, I remember, we lost a body about seven years ago. When the time for the inquest came, it could n't be found.' "

I remembered this when Mr. Yeats wrote to me lately from the Abbey: "The other day at a performance of *Countess Cathleen* one of the players stopped in the midst of his speech and it was a moment or two before he could go on. He told me afterwards his shoulder had suddenly been grasped by an invisible hand."

When the time for the opening came, I was ill and could not leave home, but had reports from him through the days before the opening. "December 24, 1904. The Company are very disappointed that you will not be up for the first night. Fay says they would all act better if you were here."

"December 20, 1904. I hear from Robert that you may get up for a little to-day. I hope you will take a long rest. I shall see about the awning for the old woman's stall to-night. Synge has a photograph, which will give us a picturesque form.

We changed all the lighting on Saturday, and the costumes look much better now. In any case everything looks so much better on the new stage. G. came in last night with a Boer, who went to Trinity, because, so far as I could make out, he thought he would find himself among sympathetic surroundings. He and some other young Boers, including one who is said to have killed more Englishmen at Spion Kop than anybody else, had to go to a university in Europe and chose Ireland. Finding the sort of place it is, they look at the situation with amusement and are trying to get out more men of their own sort to form a rebellious coterie. . . . I mention G., in order to say that he wants to try his hand at translating *Œdipus the King* for us. To-night we go on experimenting in lighting and after that will come the great problem of keeping the bottom of the trews from standing out like frilled paper at the end of a ham bone."

And finally on the very day of the opening: "December 27, '04. I am confident of a fairly good start with the plays,—the stars are quiet and fairly favourable."

Then after the first night, December 27th,

I had good telegrams and then a letter: "A great success in every way. The audience seemed 'heavy' through the opening dialogue—Fool and Blind man—and then it woke up, applauding for a long time after the exit of the kings. There was great enthusiasm at the end. *Kathleen* seemed more rebellious than I ever heard it, and —— solemnly begged me to withdraw it for fear it would stir up a conspiracy and get us all into trouble. Then came your play—a success from the first. One could hardly hear for the applause. Fay was magnificent as the melancholy man. The whole play was well played all through. I don't think I really like the stone wall wings. However, I was very near and will know better to-night. I got a beautiful light effect in *Baile's Strand*, and the audience applauded the scene even before the play began. The cottage, too, with the misty blue outside its door is lovely. We never had such an audience or such enthusiasm. The pit clapped when I came in. Our success could not have been greater. Even —— admits that your comedy [*Spreading the News*], 'is undoubtedly going to be very popular.'"

We worked for several years with Mr. W. Fay

as producer, as manager, as chief actor. In 1903, when all his time was needed for the enterprise, we paid him enough to set him free from other work, a part coming from the earnings of the Company, a part from Mr. Yeats, and a part from myself, for we had little capital at that time, outside £50 given by our good friend Mr. John Quinn, Attorney and Counsellor in New York. But even large sums of money would have been poor payment not only for William Fay's genius and his brother's beautiful speaking of verse, but for their devotion to the aim and work of the theatre, its practical and its artistic side. But they left us early in 1908 at a time of disagreement with other members, and of discouragement. I am very sorry that they, who more than almost any others had laid the foundation of the Irish Theatre, did not wait with us for its success.

But building up an audience is a slow business when there is anything unusual in the methods or the work. Often near midnight, after the theatre had closed, I have gone round to the newspaper offices, asking as a favour that notices might be put in, for we could pay for but few advertisements and it was not always thought worth while to send a critic to our plays. Often I have gone out by the stage door when the curtain was up, and come round into the auditorium by the front hall, hoping that in the dimness I might pass for a new arrival and so encourage the few scattered people in the stalls. One night there were so few in any part of the house that the players were for dismissing them and giving no performance at all. But we played after all and just after the play began, three or four priests from the country came in. A friend of theirs and of the Abbey had gone beyond the truth in telling them it was not a real theatre. They came round afterwards and told us how good they thought the work and asked the Company to come down and play in the West. Very often in the green room I have quoted the homely proverb, heard I know not where, "Grip is a good dog, but Hold Fast a better"! For there is some French blood in me that keeps my spirit up, so that I see in a letter to Mr. Yeats I am indignant at some attributions of melancholy: "I who at church last Sunday, when I heard in the Psalms 'Thou hast anointed me with the joy of gladness above my fellows', thought it must apply to me, and that some oil of the sort must have kept me watertight among seas of trouble." And Mr. Yeats in his turn wrote to encourage me in some time of attacks: "Any fool can fight a winning battle, but it needs character to fight a losing one, and that should inspire us; which reminds me that I dreamed the other night that I was being hanged, but was the life and soul of the party."

For there was not always peace inside the theatre, and there came from time to time that breaking and rebuilding that is in the course of nature, and one must think all for good in the end. And so I answered some one at a time of discord, "I am myself a lover of peace so long as it is not the peace of a dead body." And to Mr. Yeats I wrote: "I am much more angry really than you are with those who have wasted so much of your time. I look on it as child-murder. *Deirdre* might be in existence now but for this." And to one who left us but has since returned: "I want you to sit down and read Mr. Yeats's notes in the last two numbers of *Samhain* and to ask yourself if the work he is doing is best worth helping or hindering. Remember, he has been for the last eight years working with his whole heart and soul for the creation, the furtherance, the perfecting, of what he believes will be a great dramatic movement in Ireland. I have helped him all through, but we have lost many helpers by the way. Mr. Lecky, who had served us well in getting the law passed that made these dramatic experiments possible, publicly repudiated us because of Mr. Yeats's letter on the Queen's visit. . . . Others were lost for different reasons ——, ——, all of whom had been helpful in their time. Now others are dropping off. It is always sad to lose fellow-workers, but the work must go on all the same. 'No man putting his hand to the plough and drawing back is fit for the kingdom of God.' He is going on with it. I am going on with it as long as life and strength are left to me. . . . It is hard to hold one's own against those one is living amongst, I have found that; and I have found that peace comes, not from trying to please one's neighbours but in making up one's own mind what is the right path and in then keeping to it. And so God save Ireland, and believe me your sincere friend."

This now, according to my memory, is how I came to work for a National Theatre in Ireland and how that Theatre began.

CHAPTER II

THE BLESSING OF THE GENERATIONS

On the walls of the landing outside your nursery door there are pictures hanging, painted as you paint your own with water-colours, but without any blot or blur. Some are of blue hills and of streams running through brown bogs, but many of them are of young girls and of women, barefooted and wearing home-dyed clothes, knitting or carrying sheaves; or of fishermen dressed in white. All, girls and women and men alike, have gentle faces. There is no sign of the turf-smoke that dries the skin to leather. There are no lines or wrinkles to be seen. It may be faces were like that before the great famine came that changed soft bodies to skin and bone and turned villages to grazing for goats. Your great-grandfather fed his people at that time and took their sickness and died. But perhaps if that painter were living now, he would draw likenesses in the same way, with the furrows and ridges left out. For he could only see gentleness like his own in whatever he had a mind to paint.

A little lower on the staircase there are pictures you do not look at now, likenesses of men not very young, who had done something that made others like to meet them and who dined together at the Grillon Club. Your grandfather is there with many of his friends; some of them became friends of mine. Here is one that wrote books, you will maybe read them bye and bye, about good men that once lived in Ireland, and how Europe learned manners, and about witches that were thrown into ponds.

Near the library door there is a drawing of an old man. He looks very tired and sad. He was shut up in prison for more years than you have lived. He could not see the lime trees blooming out or the chestnuts breaking from their husks.

That is a younger man on the other wall. There is something like a laugh in his eyes. He will live and work a long time, I hope, for the work he has done is very good. He gave you a blessing in Irish one time when I brought him to see you in your cot.

Among the names on my first list of guarantors is that of Sir Frederic Burton, painter, and for many years Director of the National Gallery in Trafalgar Square. And this name, like that of Aubrey de Vere, brings together movements divided by half a century; for Frederic Burton had, through personal friendship with Thomas Davis, come so near to that side of the National movement of 1848 which expressed itself in writing, that he had drawn the design for the title-page of the *Spirit of the Nation*, that book of rebel songs and ballads. And he had known others of that time whose names have been remembered, Ferguson and Stokes and O'Curry. It would make my heart give a quicker beat to hear him say: "When I was in Aran with Petrie," or "my model for the Blind Girl at the Holy Well was Doctor Petrie's daughter," or "Davis was such a dear fellow I could refuse him nothing," or, as an apology for not having read Mitchell's wonderful *Gaol Journal*, "I did not like his appearance when I saw him. Davis took me to see him somewhere. He was a regular Northern and did not make a good impression on me. His skin was blotched and he had ginger-coloured hair." Though he resented the rising fame of Clarence Mangan, because, as he thought, it was at the expense of Thomas Moore, "who had—though no one would class him among the great poets—mellifluous versification, exquisite choice of language, and was endowed at least with a delicate fancy approaching to imagination," the only authentic portrait of Mangan, not taken indeed from life, but after death in an hospital, was drawn by him.

He had wandered and painted in Germany and in the west of Ireland, in Connemara and in his own county of Clare, till his work at the National Gallery forced him to give up his art. But in his last days he would often speak of his early days in the West, and of country people he remembered, a girl near Maam who was a great singer, and a piper, Paddy Conneely, who was the best judge of sheep and cattle in the whole country.

He was during the Land War when I first knew him, a very strong Unionist, for his sensitive nature shrank from its harsh and violent methods, and for a while he felt that he had no longer a country to take pride in. In 1899 he wrote: ". . . I look forward with some uneasiness to the advent of *Patriots* from beyond sea, now American citizens under the Stars and Stripes. With this outlook before it, the Government is reducing the Irish Constabulary, a most extraordinary proceeding and a quite unaccountable one except indeed on the theory that every administration is doomed to fatuity where Irish affairs have to be dealt with. For the police are the appointed guardians of civil order, and however abused or resisted, are recognised as such. But if the military have to be called out, what a handle is given to vapourers on both sides of the Irish sea! And what about the dismissed Constables? Will they not be thrown into the ranks of the Patriots?"

And in 1895 he had written, refusing an invitation to dine with me—I cannot remember who I said was coming, but he expressed this regret: "Especially as I enjoy meeting Sir A. and Lady Clay, and should have liked to see a bird so rare as an *honest* Nationalist." Yet he kept a spirit of independence that was akin to rebellion, even through those years of official position and pleasant London dinners, and friendships, and the Athenæum Club.

During the years after the death in 1892 of my husband, who had been a trustee of the National

Gallery, and Sir Frederic's death in 1900, our friendship became a close one. Our talk turned very often from pictures and Italy to Ireland. In 1897 I published *Mr. Gregory's Letter-box*, a political history of the years between 1812 and 1830, taken from letters to and by my husband's grandfather, then Under-Secretary for Ireland. Sir Frederic was much pleased with the book. He came to see me when he had read it and said: "I am glad you have come down on the real culprit, George III.," and quoted one or two people who had said his obstinacy was the cause of so many of Ireland's troubles. But after a little he said very gravely: "I see a tendency to Home Rule on your own part." I said, "I defy any one to study Irish History without getting a dislike and distrust of England." He was silent for a time and then said, "That is my feeling," and told me how patriotic he had been as a boy though disliking "O'Connell and his gang." Later he accused me of having become "A red hot Nationalist," and said I had no Irish blood, but I convinced him I had, both Irish and French.

He was as angry at the time of the Boer War as any Mayo ballad-singer or Connacht Ranger's wife. "According to the doctor I am better, but really this war is killing me. It is the worst affair I recollect. It is utterly inglorious. . . . I grieve particularly for our brave Irishmen whose lives have been squandered to no purpose." He was to the end a Unionist, so far as his political doctrine went, but I think his rooted passion for Ireland increased, and made, as such strong passions are used to do, all politics seem but accidental, transitory, a business that is outside the heart of life.

The language movement, of which I was able to bring him news, began to excite him. One day I found him "excited and incredulous at Atkinson's evidence against the Irish language, in which he says all Irish books are filthy and all folk-lore is at bottom abominable." And then he got, "on your recommendation and Doctor Hyde's reputation as a scholar" the History of Irish Literature and wrote: "I am reading Dr. Hyde's Literary History with the greatest interest. It is a high pleasure to find the matter he deals with treated by a true scholar and in a reasonable and philosophic spirit. But indeed the advance in this respect since my earlier days is marvellous. At that time the comparative method was hardly, if at all, thought of. Rabid Irishmen, who often did n't know their own language but at second hand, and knew no other tongue at all, spouted the rankest absurdities. Now true light has been let in and Irish history, archæology, literature, and poetry are the gainers. Let us not grudge to the Germans their meed of honour in having led the way." And again: "I should be exceedingly sorry if the Irish language died out of men's mouths altogether. I look upon the loss of a language or even a dialect as equivalent to the extirpation of a species in natural history. . . . " Then, in 1899: "Those addresses of Dr. Hyde and Mr. Yeats are very interesting and, I would fain hope, may find a response in the hearts of the people who heard them. The subject is one full of sadness. Self-respect, a decaying language, a dying music, how shall they be resuscitated! I could weep when I recollect how full Munster, Connacht, and even Ulster were in my earlier days of exquisite native music—when in fact among the peasantry and the Irish of the towns you heard no other; when the man at the plough-tail had his peculiar 'whistle,' strange, wild, and full of melody and rhythm. All this must now have passed away irrevocably. May the language have a better chance! I cannot tell you how much Doctor Hyde's book has moved me. Principally it is a manful effort."

When I was again in London, he showed me the Literary History close at hand and asked me a little nervously what was Douglas Hyde's age. My answer, or surmise, pleased him, and he said: "Then he will be able to work for a long time." Once or twice, when we went on to talk of other things, he came back to this and said, "I am so glad he is a young man."

He was jealous for the honour of Ireland even in lesser things. He was very much interested in the beginning of our theatre. In 1899 he writes: "I am happy to sign the guarantee form for the coming year, and enclose it. You are a dreamy lot in Erin. As you say, I think the quality comes from the atmosphere. Here there is more of the opposite than suits me, but I dream still, as I have done all my lifetime. I trust there will be no shindy at the performance of *Countess Cathleen*. But if not, our compatriots will have been for once untrue to themselves!"

And later: "I am sincerely glad the experiment was on the whole successful and that those who intended mischief after all made but a poor effort to inflict it. . . . Altogether it appears as if the old palmy days of Dublin independent appreciation of the drama were about to be revived in our altered times. I congratulate Mr. Yeats on the success of the drama as an acting piece, and in everything except —— ——'s beautiful Irish hyperbole. I recollect an account of a concert given at Clonmel several years ago, in which the eloquent local journalist said of one of the amateur lady singers, after the loftiest eulogy, 'but it was in her last song that Miss —— —— gave the *coup de grace* to her performance.' "

He cared very much for Mr. Yeats's work, but I could never persuade him to come and meet him. He always made some excuse. At last he made a promise for one afternoon, but, in place of coming, he wrote, saying he was half ashamed to confess to so much enthusiasm, but he was so much under the spell of the poems that he was afraid that, in meeting the writer, the spell might be broken. He told me when next I saw him that of the poets he had known the only ones that did not disappoint him were William Morris and Rossetti. "Swinburne was excitable; Tennyson was grumpy and posing; Browning was charming as a friend, but not fulfilling my idea of what a poet should be." But I did bring them together in the end, and he thanked me later and confessed my faith had been justified.

In 1900, during his last illness, I was often with him. I had been away in Dublin for our plays and I find a note written after my return to London: "Went to see Sir F. He is in bed, and I fear, or indeed must hope, the end is very near. . . . I went up to see him. He was clear but drowsy, at first a little inarticulate, but when I got up to go, he held my hand a long time, speaking with great kindness . . . asked for Robert, and how the plays had gone. I told him of them, and of the *Times* notice of *Maeve*, saying its idealism had been so well received by an Irish audience, and of the notice on the same page telling that *Tess* in London had been jeered at by an audience who found it too serious. He said: 'That is just what one would expect.' He asked if Robert had been abroad yet, and I said no, he was so fond of Ireland he had not cared to go until now, and that I myself found every year an increased delight and happiness in Ireland. He said, 'It is so with me. My best joys have been connected with Ireland.' Then he spoke of Celtic influence in English literature and said, 'There will some day be a great Pan-Celtic Empire.' And so we parted."

I am glad that he who had been even a little moved by that stir in the mind, that rush of revolutionary energy that moved the poets and patriots and rebels of '48, should after half a hundred years have been stirred by the intellectual energy that came with a new generation, as its imagination turned for a while from the Parliament where all was to have been set right, after the break in the Irish party and after Parnell's death.

"I enclose you a guarantee paper filled up for such a sum as I can afford (or perhaps more) to lose, but I hope there will be no loss for anybody in the matter, while there will certainly be some gain to Ireland! I 'd have answered sooner but that I am suffering from a horrible form of dyspepsia, with exceptional langour." It is no wonder if the old man who sent with this his promise for twenty shillings was somewhat broken in health. He was the last of the Fenian triumvirate,—Kickham, Luby, O'Leary,—and he had come back to Dublin after fifteen year of banishment and five of penal servitude at Portland. John O'Leary had been turning over books on the stalls by the Seine in Paris, when one day somebody had come to him and asked him to come back to Ireland where a rising was being planned, and he had come.

A part of the romance of my early days had been the whispered rumours of servants, and the overheard talk of my elders, of the threatened rising of the Fenians:

"An army of Papists grim
"With a green flag o'er them.
"Red coats and black police
"Flying before them."

The house of Roxborough, my old home, had once been attacked by Whiteboys. My father had defended it, firing from the windows, and it was not hard to believe that another attack might be made. It seemed a good occasion for being allowed to learn to shoot with my brothers, but that was in those days not thought fitting, even in self-defence, for a girl, and my gun was never loaded with anything more weighty than a coppercap. So when this new business of the theatre brought me to meet, amongst many others till then unknown, John O'Leary, I remembered those old days and the excitement of a Fenian's escape—might he not be in hiding in our own woods or hay-lofts? And I wondered to find that not only Nationalists admired and respected so wild and dangerous a rebel. So I asked Mr. Yeats to tell me the reason, for he had known him well and had even shared a lodging with him for a while; so that his friends would say: "You have the advantage over us. O'Leary takes so long to convert to any new thing, and you can begin with him at breakfast." And he wrote to me: "When John O'Leary returned from exile, he found himself in the midst of a movement which inherited the methods of O'Connell and a measure of his success. Journalists and politicians were alike in his eyes untruthful men, thinking that any means that brought the end were justified, and for that reason certain, as he thought, to miss the end desired. The root of all was, though I doubt if he put the thought into words, that journalists and politicians looked for their judges among their inferiors, and assumed those opinions and passions that moved the largest number of men. Their school is still dominant, and John O'Leary had seen through half his life, as we have seen, men coarsening their thought and their manners, and exaggerating their emotions in a daily and weekly press that was like the reverie of an hysterical woman. He was not of O'Connell's household. His master had been Davis, and he was quick to discover and condemn the man who sought for judgment not among his equals or in himself. He saw, as no one else in modern Ireland has seen, that men who make this choice are long unpopular, all through their lives it may be, but grow in sense and courage with their years, and have the most gazers even in the end.

"Yet he was not unjust to those who went the other way. He imputed to them no bad motives, for I have heard him say of a man that he distrusted, 'He would not sacrifice himself but he would risk himself,' and of a man who seemed to him to appeal always to low motives, the chief mischief-maker of his kind, 'He would sacrifice himself.' Yet, what he himself commended with his favourite word '*morale*' was the opposite of that sudden emotional self-sacrifice, the spurious heroism of popular movements, being life-long hardness and serenity, a choice made every day anew. He thought but little of opinions, even those he had sacrificed so much for, and I have heard him say, 'There was never cause so bad that it has not been defended by good men for good reasons.' And of Samuel Ferguson, poet and antiquarian, who was not of his party or any Nationalist party, 'He has been a better patriot than I.' He knew that in the end, whatever else had temporary use, it was simple things that mattered, the things a child can understand, a man's courage and his generosity.

"I do not doubt that his prison life had been hard enough, but he would not complain, having been in 'the hands of his enemies'; and he would often tell one of that life, but not of its hardships. A famous popular leader of that time, who made a great noise because he was in prison as a common felon for a political offence, made him very angry. I said 'It is well known that he has done this, not because he shrinks from hardship but because there is a danger in a popular movement that the obscure men who can alone carry it to success, may say, "our leaders are treated differently."' He answered, 'There are things a man must not do, even to save a nation.' And when I asked 'What things?' he said, 'He must not weep in public.' He knew that a doctrine expediency cries out on would have but few to follow, and he would say, 'Michael Davitt wants his converts by the thousand. I shall be satisfied with half a dozen.' Most complained of his impracticability, and there was a saying that an angel could not find a course of action he would not discover a moral flaw in, and it is probable that his long imprisonment and exile, while heightening his sense of ideal law, had deprived him of initiative by taking away its opportunities. He would often complain that the young men would not follow him, and I once said, 'Your power is that they do not. We can do nothing till we have converted you; you are our conscience.' Yet he lived long enough to see the young men grow to middle life and assume like their fathers before them that a good Irishman is he who agreed with the people. Yet we, when we withstand the people, owe it to him that we can feel we have behind us an Irish tradition. 'My religion,' he would say, 'is the old Persian one, "To pull the bow and speak the truth." '

"I do not know whether he would have liked our unpopular plays, but I cannot imagine him growing excited because he thought them slanders upon Ireland. O'Connell had called the Irish peasantry the finest peasantry upon earth, and his heirs found it impossible to separate patriotism and flattery. Again and again John O'Leary would return to this, and I have heard him say, 'I think it probable that the English national character is finer than ours, but that does not make me want to be an Englishman.' I have often heard him defend Ireland against one charge or another, and he was full of knowledge, but the patriotism he had sacrificed so much for marred neither his justice nor his scholarship.

"He disapproved of much of Parnell's policy, but Parnell was the only man in Irish public life of his day who had his sympathy, and I remember hearing some one say in those days before the split that are growing vague to me, that Parnell never came to Dublin without seeing him. They were perhaps alike in some hidden root of character though the one had lived a life of power and excitement, while the other had been driven into contemplation by circumstance and as I think by nature. Certainly they were both proud men."

He was, when I knew him, living in a little room, books all around him and books in heaps upon the floor. I would send him sometimes snipe or golden plover from Kiltartan bog or woodcock from the hazel woods at Coole, hoping to tempt him with something that might better nourish the worn body than the little custard pudding that was used to serve him for his two days' dinner, because of that "horrible dyspepsia" that often makes those who have been long in prison live starving after their release, mocked with the sight of food.

It was through reading Davis's poems he had become a Nationalist, and his own influence had helped to shape this other poet in the same fashion, for from the time of Yeats's boyhood there had been a close friendship between them, the old man admiring the young man's genius, and taking his side in the quarrels that arose about patriotism in poetry and the like. I remember their both dining with me one evening in London and coming on to see a very poor play, very badly acted by some Irish society. At its end Yeats was asked to say some words of gratitude for the performance, during which we had all felt impatient and vexed. He did speak at some length, and held his audience, and without telling any untruth left them feeling that all had gone well. John O'Leary turned to me and said fervently, "I don't think there is anything on God's earth that Willie Yeats could not make a speech about!"

There is a bust of John O'Leary in the Municipal Gallery. The grand lines of the massive head, the eyes full of smouldering fire, might be those of some ancient prophet understanding his people's doom.

There is nothing of storm or unrest about that other Dublin monument, that bronze figure sitting tranquilly within the gates of Trinity College and within its quadrangle. Lecky was the reasoner, the philosopher, the looker-on, writing his histories, even of Ireland, through the uproar of the Land War with the same detachment as did the Four Masters, writing their older history amongst the wars and burnings of the seventeenth century that were so terrible in Ireland.

He had been a debater while an undergraduate of Trinity, and it was fitting that he should have represented it in Parliament during his last years.

Trinity, where Wolfe Tone had been an undergraduate a hundred years earlier had changed in that hundred years. I was in Paris in 1900 and went to see an old acquaintance, that most imaginative archæologist, Salomon Reinach. He told me he had been lately to Ireland and he had been astonished by two things, the ignorance of the Irish language—it was not known even by the head of the Dublin Museum or the head of its archæological side—and by the hostility of Trinity College to all things Irish. "It is an English fort, nothing else." "Its garrison," the students, had gone out and broken the windows of a newspaper office while he was there, and he had spent an evening with Doctor Mahaffy, who was "much astonished that I was no longer taken up with Greek things, and that I found Irish antiquity so much more interesting."

I have already told of Lecky's help to our theatre. He had a real affection for his country but was not prone to join societies or leagues. He had given us his name as one of our first guarantors, offering £5 instead of the £1 I had asked. But he publicly withdrew his name later, without his usual reasonableness, because of letters written by Mr. Yeats and Mr. George Moore at the time of Queen Victoria's visit to Dublin. This had been announced as a private visit, and Nationalists had promised a welcome. Then it was turned into a public one, and there was a good deal of angry feeling, and it seemed as if the theatre—although quite outside politics—would suffer for a while. Though Mr. Yeats, wrote: "I don't think you need be anxious about next year's theatre. Clever Unionists will take us on our merits, and the rest would never like us at any time. I have found a greatly increased friendliness on the part of some of the younger men here. In a battle like Ireland's, which is one of poverty against wealth, one must prove one's sincerity by making oneself unpopular to wealth. One must accept the baptism of the gutter. Have not all teachers done the like?" I answered that I preferred the baptism of clean water. I was troubled by the misunderstanding of friends.

Trinity College is not keeping aloof now, and as to Mr. Lecky himself, the House of Commons took away some prejudices. He spoke to me of Mr. John Redmond and his leadership with great admiration and esteem. I find a note written after a pleasant dinner with him and Mrs. Lecky in Onslow Gardens: "He grieved over the exaggerated statements of the financial reformers. I pressed Land Purchase as the solution of our trouble, but he says what is true, 'It means changing every hundred pounds into seventy.' Talking of Robert's future, he said, 'It is a great thing to have a competence behind one.' He said he had been brought up for the Church, but found he could not enter it, and went abroad and drifted, never thinking he would marry, and leading a solitary life, and so took to letters and succeeded. He thinks Parliament lessens one's interest in political questions,—so much connected with them is of no value, and there is so much empty noise."

I often heard of his speaking well and even boasting of our Theatre and its work, but though he often came to see me, he would not quite give up fault-finding. "Dined at Lecky's; he rather cross.

He took me down to dinner and said first thing, 'What silly speeches your Celtic people have been making.' 'Moore?' I asked. 'Yes, and Yeats. Oh, very silly!' He is in bad humour because Blackrock, which he has known, and known to speak English all his life, has sent him a copy of resolutions in favour of the revival of Irish. In revenge I told him how a Deputy Lieutenant (Edward Martyn) was proclaiming himself a convert to Nationalism through reading his *Leaders of Public Opinion in Ireland.* But that book, he used to say, had been a long time in influencing anybody, for of its first edition only thirty copies had been sold."

He forgave us all after a while, used to come and ask for news whenever I had come to London from home, and told me quite proudly after a visit to Oxford that the undergraduates there accepted no living poet but Yeats. But to the last he would say to me plaintively on parting, "Do not do anything incendiary when you go back to Ireland."

My first meeting with Douglas Hyde had been when he came in one day with a broken bicycle during lunch at my neighbour Mr. Martyn's house where I was staying. He had been coming by train, but had got out at a village, Craughwell (as I myself did a good while afterwards on the same errand), in search of memories of Raftery, the Connacht poet. I had my own pony carriage with me, and that afternoon I drove to the Round Tower and the seven churches of Kilmacduagh, taking with me Douglas Hyde and Mr. William Sharp, whom I even then suspected of being "Fiona Macleod." Mr. Sharp—not by my invitation—took the place beside me, and left the back seat for the poet-dramatist, the founder of the Gaelic League of Ireland.

He often came to stay with me and my son at Coole after that. The first time was in winter, for a shooting party. Some old ladies—our neighbours—asked our keeper who our party was, and on hearing that one was a gentleman who spoke to the beaters in Irish, they said, "he can not be a gentleman if he speaks Irish." With all his culture and learning, his delight was in talking with the people and hearing their poems and fragments of the legends. I remember one day, he went into a thatched cottage to change his boots after shooting snipe on Kilmacduagh bog, and talked with an old woman who had not much English and who welcomed him when he spoke in her own tongue. But when she heard he was from Mayo, looked down on by dwellers in Galway, she laughed very much and repeated a line of a song in Irish which runs:

"There 'll be boots on me yet, says the man from the county Mayo!"

Near Kilmacduagh also he was told a long story, having Aristotle for its hero. Sometimes he was less lucky. I brought an old man to see him, I was sure could give him stories. But he only told one of a beggar who went to Castle ——, a neighbouring house, the master of which had given him a half-penny, saying, "that is for my father's and mother's soul." "And the beggar added another half-penny to it, and laid it down on the step, and, 'There 's a half-penny for my father's soul and a half-penny for my mother's, and I would n't go to the meanness of putting them both in one.'"

He has done his work by methods of peace, by keeping quarrels out of his life, with all but entire success. I find in a letter to Mr. Yeats: "I will send you Claideam that you may see some of the attacks by recalcitrant Gaelic Leaguers on the Craoibhin. Well, I am sorry, but if he can't keep from making enemies, what chance is there for the like of us?"

He was one of the vice-presidents of our Society for a while and we are always grateful to him for that *Twisting of the Rope* in which he played with so much gaiety, ease, and charm. But in founding the Gaelic League, he had done far more than that for our work. It was a movement for keeping the Irish language a spoken one, with, as a chief end, the preserving of our own nationality. That does not sound like the beginning of a revolution, yet it was one. It was the discovery, the disclosure of the folk-learning, the folk-poetry, the folk-tradition. Our Theatre was caught into that current, and it is that current, as I believe, that has brought it on its triumphant way. It is chiefly known now as a folk-theatre. It has not only the great mass of primitive material and legend to draw on, but it has been made a living thing by the excitement of that discovery. All our writers, Mr. Yeats himself, were influenced by it. Mr. Synge found what he had lacked before—fable, emotion, style. Writing of him I have said "He tells what he owes to that collaboration with the people, and for all the attacks, he has given back to them what they will one day thank him for. . . . The return to the people, the reunion after separation, the taking and giving, is it not the perfect circle, the way of nature, the eternal wedding-ring?"

CHAPTER III

PLAY-WRITING

WHEN we first planned our Theatre, there were very few plays to choose from, but our faith had no bounds and as the Irish proverb says, "When the time comes, the child comes."

The plays that I have cared for most all through, and for love of which I took up this work, are those verse ones by Mr. Yeats *The Countess Cathleen* with which we began, *The Shadowy Waters*, *The King's Threshold*, and the rest. They have sometimes seemed to go out of sight because the prose plays are easier to put on and to take from place to place; yet they will always be, if I have my way, a part of our year's work. I feel verse is more than any prose can be, the apex of the flame, the point of the diamond. The well-to-do people in our stalls sometimes say, "We have had enough of verse plays, give us comedy." But the people in the sixpenny places do not say they get too much of them, and the players themselves work in them with delight. I wrote to Mr. Yeats when *On Baile's Strand* was being rehearsed: "Just back from rehearsal, and cheered up on the whole. The Molière goes very well, and will be quite safe when the two servants have been given a little business. Synge says it was quite different to-night. They all waked up in honour of me. As to *Baile's Strand*, it will be splendid. . . . The only real blot at present is the song, and it is very bad. The three women repeat it together. Their voices don't go together. One gets nervous listening for the separate ones. No one knows how you wish it done. Every one thinks the words ought to be heard. I got Miss Allgood to speak it alone, and that was beautiful, and we thought if it did n't delay the action too long, she might speak it, and at the end she and the others might sing or hum some lines of it to a definite tune. If you can quite decide what should be done, you can send directions, but if you are doubtful, I almost think you must come over. You must n't risk spoiling the piece. It is quite beautiful. W. Fay most enthusiastic, says you are a wonderful man, and keeps repeating lines. He says,

'There is nothing like that being written in London.'"

But the listeners, and this especially when they are lovers of verse, have to give so close an attention to the lines, even when given their proper value and rhythm as by our players, that ear and mind crave ease and unbending, and so comedies were needed to give this rest. That is why I began writing them, and it is still my pride when one is thought worthy to be given in the one evening with the poetic work.

I began by writing bits of dialogue, when wanted. Mr. Yeats used to dictate parts of *Diarmuid and Grania* to me, and I would suggest a sentence here and there. Then I, as well as another, helped to fill spaces in *Where There is Nothing*. Mr. Yeats says in dedicating it to me: "I offer you a book which is in part your own. Some months ago, when our Irish dramatic movement took its present form, I saw that somebody must write a number of plays in prose if it was to have a good start. I did not know what to do, although I had my dramatic fables ready and a pretty full sketch of one play, for my eyes were troubling me, and I thought I could do nothing but verse, which one can carry

Miss Sara Allgood

From a drawing by Robert Gregory

about in one's head for a long time, and write down, as De Musset put it, with a burnt match. You said I might dictate to you, and we worked in the mornings at Coole, and I never did anything that went so easily and quickly; for when I hesitated you had the right thought ready and it was almost always you who gave the right turn to the phrase and gave it the ring of daily life. We finished several plays, of which this is the longest, in so few weeks that if I were to say how few, I do not think anybody would believe me."

Where There is Nothing was given by the Stage Society in London, but Mr. Yeats was not satisfied with it, and we have since re-written it as *The Unicorn from the Stars*. Yet it went well and was vital. It led to an unexpected result: "I hear that some man of a fairly respectable class was taken up with a lot of tinkers somewhere in Munster, and that the Magistrate compared him to 'Paul Ruttledge.' The next night one of the tinkers seems to have said something to the others about their being in a book. The others resented this in some way, and there was a fight, which brought them all into Court again. I am trying to get the papers."

Later in the year we wrote together *Kathleen ni Houlihan* and to that he wrote an introductory letter addressed to me: "One night I had a dream almost as distinct as a vision, of a cottage where there was well-being and firelight and talk of a marriage, and into the midst of that cottage there came an old woman in a long cloak. She was Ireland herself, that Kathleen ni Houlihan for whom so many songs have been sung and for whose sake so many have gone to their death. I thought if I could write this out as a little play, I could make others see my dream as I had seen it, but I could not get down from that high window of dramatic verse, and in spite of all you had done for me, I had not the country speech. One has to live among the people, like you, of whom an old man said in my hearing, 'She has been a serving maid among us,' before one can think the thoughts of the people and speak with their tongue. We turned my dream into the little play, *Kathleen ni Houlihan*, and when we gave it to the little theatre in Dublin and found that the working people liked it, you helped me to put my other dramatic fables into speech."

For *The Pot of Broth* also I wrote dialogue and

I worked as well at the plot and the construction of some of the poetic plays, especially *The King's Threshold* and *Deirdre;* for I had learned by this time a good deal about play-writing to which I had never given thought before. I had never cared much for the stage, although when living a good deal in London, my husband and I went, as others do, to see some of each season's plays. I find, in looking over an old diary, that many of these have quite passed from my mind, although books I read ever so long ago, novels and the like, have left at least some faint trace by which I may recognise them.

We thought at our first start it would make the whole movement more living and bring it closer to the people if the Gaelic League would put on some plays written in Irish. Dr. Hyde thought well of the idea, and while staying here at Coole, as he did from time to time, he wrote *The Twisting of the Rope*, based on one of Mr. Yeats's Hanrahan stories; *The Lost Saint* on a legend given its shape by Mr. Yeats, and *The Nativity* on a scenario we wrote together for him. Afterwards he wrote *The Marriage* and *The Poorhouse*, upon in each case a scenario written by me. I betray no secret in telling this, for Dr. Hyde has made none of the collaboration, giving perhaps too generous acknowledgment, as in Galway, where he said, when called before the curtain after *The Marriage*, that the play was not his but that Lady Gregory had written it and brought it to him, saying "*Cur Gaedilge air*," "Put Irish on it." I find in a letter of mine to Mr. Yeats: "Thanks for sending back Raftery. I have n't sent it to Hyde yet. The real story was that Raftery by chance went into a house where such a wedding was taking place 'that was only a marriage and not a wedding' and where there was 'nothing but a herring for the dinner,' and he made a song about it and about all the imaginary grand doings at it that has been remembered ever since. But it did n't bring any practical good to the young people, for Raftery himself 'had to go to bed in the end without as much as a drop to drink, but he did n't mind that, where they had n't it to give.' "

But it went through some changes after that: "I have a letter from the Craoibhin. He has lost his Trinity College play and must re-write it from my translation. He is not quite satisfied with

Raftery (*The Marriage*). 'I don't think Maire's uncertainty if it be a ghost or not is effective on the stage. I would rather have the ghost "out and out" as early as possible, and make it clear to the audience.' I rather agree with him. I think I will restore the voice at the door in my published version."

And again I wrote from Galway: "I came here yesterday for a few days' change, but the journey, or the little extra trouble at leaving, set my head aching, and I had to spend all yesterday in a dark room. In the evening, when the pain began to go, I began to think of the Raftery play, and I want to know if this end would do. After the miser goes out, Raftery stands up and says, 'I won't be the only one in the house to give no present to the woman of the house,' and hands her the plate of money, telling them to count it. While they are all gathered round counting it, he slips quietly from the door. As he goes out, wheels or horse steps are heard, and a farmer comes in and says, 'What is going on? All the carts of the country gathered at the door, and Seaghan, the Miser, going swearing down the road?' They say it is a wedding party called in by Raftery. But where is Raftery? Is he gone? They ask the farmer if he met him outside—the poet Raftery—and he says, 'I did not, but I stood by his grave at Killeenin yesterday.' Do you think that better? It gets rid of the good-byes and the storm, and I don't think any amount of hints convey the ghostly idea strongly enough. Let me know at once; just a word will do."

As to *The Poorhouse*, the idea came from a visit to Gort Workhouse one day when I heard that the wife of an old man, who had been long there, maimed by something, a knife I think, that she had thrown at him in a quarrel, had herself now been brought in to the hospital. I wondered how they would meet, as enemies or as friends, and I thought it likely they would be glad to end their days together for old sake's sake. This is how I wrote down my fable: "Scene, ward of a workhouse; two beds containing the old men; they are quarrelling. Occupants of other invisible beds are heard saying, 'There they are at it again; they are always quarrelling.' They say the matron will be coming to call for order, but another says the matron has been sent for to see somebody who wants to remove one of the paupers.

Both old men wish they could be removed from each other and have the whole ridge of the world between them. The fight goes on. One old man tells the other that he remembers the time he used to be stealing ducks, and he a boy at school. The other old man remembers the time his neighbour was suspected of going to Souper's school, etc., etc. They remember the crimes of each other's lives. They fight like two young whelps that go on fighting till they are two old dogs. At last they take their pillows and throw them at each other. Other paupers (invisible) cheer and applaud. Then they take their porringers, pipes, prayer-books, or whatever is in reach, to hurl at each other. They lament the hard fate that has put them in the same ward for five years and in beds next each other for the last three months, and they after being enemies the whole of their lives. Suddenly a cry that the matron is coming. They settle themselves hurriedly. Each puts his enemy's pillow under his head and lies down. The matron comes in with a countrywoman comfortably dressed. She embraces one old man. She is his sister. Her husband died from her lately and she is lonesome and does n't like to think of her brother being in the workhouse. If he is bedridden itself, he would be company for her. He is delighted, asks what sort of house she has. She says, a good one, a nice kitchen, and he can be doing little jobs for her. He can be sitting in a chair beside the fire and stirring the stirabout for her and throwing a bit of food to the chickens when she is out in the field. He asks when he can go. She says she has the chance of a lift for him on a neighbour's cart. He can come at once. He says he will make no delay. A loud sob from the old man in the other bed. He says, 'Is it going away you are, you that I knew through all my lifetime, and leaving me among strangers?' The first old man asks his sister if she will bring him too. She is indignant, says she won't. First old man says maybe he 'd be foolish to go at all. How does he know if he 'd like it. She says, he is to please himself; if he does n't come, she can easily get a husband, having, as she has, a nice way of living, and three lambs going to the next market. The first man says, well, he won't go; if she would bring the other old man, he would go. She turns her back angrily. Paupers in other beds call out she 'll find a good husband amongst them. She pulls on her shawl scornfully to go away. She gives her brother one more chance; he says he won't go. She says good-bye and bad luck to him. She leaves. He says that man beyond would be lonesome with no one to contradict him. The other man says he would not. The first man says, 'You want some one to be arguing with you always.' The second man, 'I do not.' The first man says, 'You are at your lies again.' The second takes up his pillow to heave at him again. Curtain falls on two men arming themselves with pillows."

I intended to write the full dialogue myself, but Mr. Yeats thought a new Gaelic play more useful for the moment, and rather sadly I laid that part of the work upon Dr. Hyde. It was all for the best in the end, for the little play, when we put it on at the Abbey, did not go very well. It seemed to ravel out into loose ends, and we did not repeat it; nor did the Gaelic players like it as well as *The Marriage* and *The Lost Saint*. After a while, when the Fays had left us, I wanted a play that would be useful to them, and with Dr. Hyde's full leave I re-wrote the *Poorhouse* as *The Workhouse Ward*. I had more skill by that time, and it was a complete re-writing, for the two old men in the first play had been talking at an imaginary audience of other old men in the ward. When this was done away with the dialogue became of necessity more closely knit, more direct and personal, to the great advantage of the play, although it was rejected as "too local" by the players for whom I had written it. The success of this set me to cutting down the number of parts in later plays until I wrote *Grania* with only three persons in it, and *The Bogie Men* with only two. I may have gone too far, and have, I think, given up an intention I at one time had of writing a play for a man and a scarecrow only, but one has to go on with experiment or interest in creation fades, at least so it is with me.

In 1902, my *Twenty-five* was staged; a rather sentimental comedy, not very amusing. It was useful at the time when we had so few, but it was weak, ending, as did for the most part the Gaelic plays that began to be written, in a piper and a dance. I tried to get rid of it afterwards by writing *The Jackdaw* on the same idea, but in which I make humour lay the ghost of sentiment. But *Twenty-five* may yet be rewritten and come to a little life of its own. *Spreading the News* was played at the opening of the Abbey Theatre, December 27, 1904. I heard it attacked at that time on the ground that Irish people never were gossips to such an extent, but it has held its own, and our audiences have had their education as well as writers and players, and know now that a play is a selection not a photograph and that the much misquoted "mirror to nature" was not used by its author or any good play-writer at all.

Perhaps I ought to have written nothing but these short comedies, but desire for experiment is like fire in the blood, and I had had from the beginning a vision of historical plays being sent by us through all the counties of Ireland. For to have a real success and to come into the life of the country, one must touch a real and eternal emotion, and history comes only next to religion in our country. And although the realism of our young writers is taking the place of fantasy and romance in the cities, I still hope to see a little season given up every year to plays on history and in sequence at the Abbey, and I think schools and colleges may ask to have them sent and played in their halls, as a part of the day's lesson. I began with the daring and lightheartedness of a schoolboy to write a tragedy in three acts upon a great personality, Brian the High King. I made many bad beginnings, and if I had listened to Mr. Yeats's advice I should have given it up, but I began again and again till it was at last moulded in at least a possible shape. It went well with our audience. There was some enthusiasm for it, being the first historical play we had produced. An old farmer came up all the way from Kincora, the present Killaloe, to see it, and I heard he went away sad at the tragic ending. He said, "Brian ought not to have married that woman. He should have been content with a nice, quiet girl from his own district." For stormy treacherous Gormleith of many husbands had stirred up the battle that brought him to his death. *Dervorgilla* I wrote at a time when circumstances had forced us to accept an English stage-manager for the Abbey. I was very strongly against this. I felt as if I should be spoken of some day as one who had betrayed her country's trust. I wrote so vehemently and sadly to Mr. Yeats about it that he might have been moved from the path of expediency, which I now think was the wise one, had the letter reached him in time, but it lay with others in the Kiltartan letter-box during a couple of weeks, Christmas time or the wintry weather giving an excuse to the mail-car driver whose duty it is to clear the box as he nightly passed it by. So he wrote: "I think we should take Vedrenne's recommendation unless we have some strong reason to the contrary. If the man is not Irish, we cannot help it. If the choice is between filling our country's stomach or enlarging its brains by importing precise knowledge, I am for scorning its stomach for the present. . . . I should have said that I told Vedrenne that good temper is essential, and he said the man he has recommended is a vegetarian and that Bernard Shaw says that vegetables are wonderful for the temper."

Mr. Synge had something of my feeling about alien management. He wrote later: "The first show of —— was deplorable. It came out as a bastard literary pantomime, put on with many of the worst tricks of the English stage. That is the end of all the Samhain principles and this new tradition that we were to lay down! I felt inclined to walk out of the Abbey and go back no more. The second Saturday was much less offensive. —— is doing his best obviously and he may perhaps in time come to understand our methods."

To come back to play-writing, I find in a letter to Mr. Yeats. "You will be amused to hear that although, or perhaps because, I had evolved out of myself 'Mr. Quirke' as a conscious philanthropist, an old man from the workhouse told me two days ago that he had been a butcher of Quirke's sort and was quite vainglorious about it, telling me how many staggery sheep and the like he had killed, that would, if left to die, have been useless or harmful. 'But I often stuck a beast and it kicking yet and life in it, so that it could do no harm to a Christian or a dog or an animal.'" And later: "Yet another 'Mr. Quirke' has been to see me. He says there are no sick pigs now, because they are all sent off to . . . no, I must n't give the address. Has not a purgatory been imagined where writers find themselves surrounded by the characters they have created?"

The *Canavans*, as I say in a note to it, was

"written I think less by logical plan than in one of those moments of lightheartedness that, as I think, is an inheritance from my great-grandmother Frances Algoin, a moment of that 'sudden Glory, the Passion which maketh those Grimaces called Laughter.' Some call it farce, some like it the best of my comedies. This very day, October 16th, I have been sent a leaf from the examination papers of the new University, in which the passage chosen from literature to 'put Irish on' is that speech of Peter Canavan's beginning. 'Would any one now think it a thing to hang a man for, that he had striven to keep himself safe?'"

But we never realise our dreams. I think it was *The Full Moon* that was in the making when I wrote: "I am really getting to work on a little comedy, of which I think at present that if its feet are of clay, its high head will be of rubbed gold, and that people will stop and dance when they hear it and not know for a while the piping was from beyond the world! But no doubt if it ever gets acted, it will be 'what Lady Gregory calls a comedy and everybody else, a farce!'"

The *Deliverer* is a crystallising of the story, as the people tell it, of Parnell's betrayal. Only yesterday some beggar from Crow Lane, the approach to Gort, told me he heard one who had been Parnell's friend speak against him at the time of the split: "He brought down O'Shea's wife on him and said he was not fit to be left at large. The people did n't like that and they hooted him and he was vexed and said he could buy up the whole of them for half a glass of porter!" I may look on *The Rising of the Moon* as an historical play, as my history goes, for the scene is laid in the historical time of the rising of the Fenians in the sixties. But the real fight in the play goes on in the sergeant's own mind, and so its human side makes it go as well in Oxford or London or Chicago as in Ireland itself. But Dublin Castle finds in it some smell of rebellion and has put us under punishment for its sins. When we came back from America last March, we had promised to give a performance on our first day in Dublin and *The Rising of the Moon* was one of the plays announced. But the stage costumes had not yet arrived, and we sent out to hire some from a depot from which the cast uniforms of the Constabulary may be lent out to the companies performing at the theatres—the Royal, the Gaiety, and the Queens.

But our messenger came back empty-handed. An order had been issued by the authorities that "no clothes were to be lent to the Abbey because *The Rising of the Moon* was derogatory to His Majesty's forces." So we changed the bill and put on the *Workhouse Ward*, in which happily a quilt and blanket cover any deficiency of clothes.

We wanted to put on some of Molière's plays. They seemed akin to our own. But when one translation after another was tried, it did not seem to carry, to "go across the footlights." So I tried putting one into our own Kiltartan dialect, *The Doctor in Spite of Himself*, and it went very well. I went on, therefore, and translated *Scapin* and *The Miser*. Our players give them with great spirit; the chief parts—Scapin, Harpagon, and Frosine—could hardly be bettered in any theatre. I confess their genius does not suit so well the sentimental and artificial young lovers.

Mr. Yeats wrote from Paris: "Dec. 19, '08, I saw two days ago a performance of *Scapin* at the Odeon. I really like our own better. It seemed to me that a representation so traditional in its type as that at the Odeon has got too far from life, as we see it, to give the full natural

7

pleasure of comedy. It was much more farcical than anything we have ever done. I have recorded several pieces of new business and noted costumes which were sometimes amusing. The acting was amazingly skilful and everything was expressive in the extreme. I noticed one difference between this production and ours which almost shocked me, so used am I to our own ways. There were cries of pain and real tears. Scapin cried when his master threatened him in the first act, and the old man, beaten by the supposed bully, was obviously very sore. I have always noticed that with our people there is never real suffering even in tragedy. One felt in the French comedians an undercurrent of passion—passion which our people never have. I think we give in comedy a kind of fancifulness and purity."

It is the existence of the Theatre that has created play-writing among us. Mr. Boyle had written stories, and only turned to plays when he had seen our performances in London. Mr. Colum claimed to have turned to drama for our sake, and Mr. Fitzmaurice, Mr. Ray, and Mr. Murray—a National schoolmaster—would certainly not have written but for that chance of having their work acted. A. E. wrote to me: "I think the Celtic Theatre will emerge all right, for if it is not a manifest intention of the gods that there should be such a thing, why the mania for writing drama which is furiously absorbing our Irish writers?" And again almost sadly: "Would it be inconvenient for me to go to Coole on Monday next . . . ? I am laying in a stock of colours and boards for painting and hope the weather will keep up. I hear Synge is at Coole, and as an astronomer of human nature, calculating the probable effect of one heavenly body on another which is invisible, I suppose W. B. Y. is at drama again and that the summer of verse is given over."

I asked Mr. Lennox Robinson how he had begun, and he said he had seen our players in Cork, and had gone away thinking of nothing else than to write a play for us to produce. He wrote and sent us *The Clancy Name*. We knew nothing of him, but saw there was good stuff in the play, and sent it back with suggestions for strengthening it and getting rid of some unnecessary characters. He altered it and we put it on. Then he wrote a three-act play *The Cross Roads*, but after he had seen it played he took away the first act, making it a far better play, for it is by seeing one's work on the stage that one learns best. Then he wrote *Harvest* with three strong acts, and this year *Patriots*, which has gone best of all.

One of our heaviest tasks had been reading the plays sent in. For some years Mr. Yeats and I read every one of these; but now a committee reports on them first and sends back those that are quite impossible with a short printed notice:

"The Reading Committee of the National Theatre Society regret to say that the enclosed play, which you kindly submitted to them, is, for various reasons, not suitable for production by the Abbey Company."

If a play is not good enough to produce, but yet shows some skill in construction or dialogue, we send another printed form written by Mr. Yeats:

"ADVICE TO PLAYWRIGHTS WHO ARE SENDING PLAYS TO THE ABBEY, DUBLIN

The Abbey Theatre is a subsidised theatre with an educational object. It will, therefore, be useless as a rule to send it plays intended as popular entertainments and that alone, or originally written for performance by some popular actor at the popular theatres. A play to be suitable for performance at the Abbey should contain some criticism of life, founded on the experience or personal observation of the writer, or some vision of life, of Irish life by preference, important from its beauty or from some excellence of style; and this intellectual quality is not more necessary to tragedy than to the gayest comedy.

"We do not desire propagandist plays, nor plays written mainly to serve some obvious moral purpose; for art seldom concerns itself with those interests or opinions that can be defended by argument, but with realities of emotion and character that become self-evident when made vivid to the imagination.

"The dramatist should also banish from his mind the thought that there are some ingredients, the love-making of the popular stage for instance, especially fitted to give dramatic pleasure; for any knot of events, where there is passionate emotion and clash of will, can be made the subject matter of a play, and the less like a play it is at the first sight the better play may come of it in the end. Young writers should remember that they must get all their effects from the logical expression of their subject, and not by the addition of extraneous incidents; and that a work of art can have but one subject. A work of art, though it must have the effect of nature, is art because it is not nature, as Goethe said: and it must possess a unity unlike the accidental profusion of nature.

"The Abbey Theatre is continually sent plays which show that their writers have not understood that the attainment of this unity by what is usually a long shaping and reshaping of the plot, is the principal labour of the dramatist, and not the writing of the dialogue.

"Before sending plays of any length, writers would often save themselves some trouble by sending a 'Scenario,' or scheme of the plot, together with one completely written act and getting the opinion of the Reading Committee as to its suitability before writing the whole play.

I find a note from Mr. Yeats: "Some writer offers us a play which 'unlike those at the Abbey,' he says, is so constructed as to admit any topic or a scene laid in any country. It will under the circumstances, he says, 'do good to all.' I am sending him 'Advice to Playwrights.' "

The advice was not always gratefully received. I wrote to Mr. Yeats: "Such an absurd letter in the *Cork Sportsman*, suggesting that you make all other dramatists rewrite their plays to hide your own idiosyncrasy!"

If a play shows real promise and a mind behind it, we write personally to the author, making criticisms and suggestions. We were accused for a while of smothering the work of young writers in order that we might produce our own, but time has done away with that libel, and we are very proud of the school of drama that has come into being through the creation of our Theatre. We were advised also to put on more popular work, work that would draw an audience for the moment from being topical, or because the author had friends in some league. But we went on giving what we thought good until it became popular. I wrote once, thinking we had yielded over much: "I am sorry ——'s play has been so coldly received (a play that has since become a favourite one), but I think it is partly our own fault. It would have got a better welcome a year ago. We have been humouring our audience instead of educating it, which is the work we ought to do. It is not only giving so much —— and ——, it is the want of good work pressed on, and I believe the want of verse, which they respect anyhow. . . . I think the pressing on of Synge's two plays the best thing we can do for this season. We have a great backing now in his reputation. In the last battle, when we cried up his genius, we were supposed to do it for our own interest. . . . I only read Gerothwohl's speech after you left, and thought that sentence most excellent about the theatre he was connected with being intended 'for art and a thinking Democracy.' It is just what we set out to do, and now we are giving in to stupidity in a Democracy. I think the sentence should be used when we can."

One at least of the many gloomy prophecies written to Mr. Yeats at some time of trouble has not come true: "I am giving you the situation as it appears to me. Remember there is —— and —— and —— An amalgamation of all the dissentients with a Gaelic dramatic society would leave Synge, Lady Gregory, and Boyle with yourself, and none of these have drawing power in Dublin. . . . You who initiated the theatre movement in Ireland, will be out of it."

Neither Mr. Yeats nor I take the writing of our plays lightly. We work hard to get clearly both fable and idea. *The Travelling Man* was first my idea and then we wrote it together. Then Mr. Yeats wrote a variant of it as a Pagan play, *The Black Horse*, and to this we owe the song, "There 's many a strong farmer whose heart would break in two." It did not please him however, and then I worked it out in my own way. I wrote to him: "I am not sure about your idea, for if the Stranger wanted the child to be content with the things near him, why did he make the image of the Garden of Paradise and ride to it? I am more inclined to think the idea is the soul having once seen the Christ, the Divine Essence, must always turn back to it again. One feels sure the child will though all its life. And the mother, with all her comforts, has never been quite satisfied, because she wants to see the Christ again. But the earthly side of her built up the dresser, and the child will build up other earthly veils; yet never be quite satisfied. What do you think?"

And again: "I am trying so hard to get to work on a play and first excuses came—Thursday headache; now I feel myself longing to take over the saw-mill, which has stopped with the head sawyer's departure and only wants a steady superintendent; or to translate *L'Avare* or the Irish fairy tales, or anything rather than creative work! You feel just the same with the Theatre; anything that is more or less external administration is so easy! Why were we not born to be curators of museums?"

At another time he writes: "Every day up to this I have worked at my play in the greatest gloom and this morning half the time was the worst yet—all done against the grain. I had half decided to throw it aside, till I had got back my belief in myself with some sheer poetry. When I began, I got some philosophy and my mind became abundant and therefore cheerful. If I can make it obey my own definition of tragedy, passion defined by motives, I shall be all right. I was trying for too much character. If, as I think you said, farce is comedy with character left out, melodrama is, I believe, tragedy with passion left out."

As to our staging of plays, in 1903, the costumes for *The Hour-Glass* were designed by my son, and from that time a great deal of the work was done by him. *The Hour-Glass* dresses were purple played against a green curtain. It was our first attempt at the decorative staging long demanded by Mr. Yeats. Mr. Yeats says, in *Samhain*, 1905, "Our staging of *Kincora*, the work of Mr. Robert Gregory, was beautiful, with a high grave dignity and that strangeness which Ben Jonson thought to be a part of all excellent beauty."

The first acts of the play are laid in King Brian's great hall at Kincora. It was hung with green curtains, there were shields embossed with designs in gold upon the walls, and heavy mouldings over the doors. The last act showed Brian's tent at Clontarf; a great orange curtain filled the background, and it is hard to forget the effect at the end of three figures standing against it, in green, in red, in grey. For a front scene there was a curtain—we use it still in its dimness and age—with a pattern of tree stems interlaced and of leaves edged with gold. This was the most costly staging we had yet attempted: it came with costumes to £30. A great deal of unpaid labour went into it.

Mr. Fay discovered a method of making papier mâché, a chief part of which seemed to be the boiling down of large quantities of our old programmes, for the mouldings and for the shields. I have often seen the designer himself on his knees by a great iron pot—one we use in cottage scenes—dying pieces of sacking, or up high on a ladder painting his forests or leaves. His staging of *The Shadowy Waters* was almost more beautiful; the whole stage is the sloping deck of a galley, blue and dim, the sails and dresses are green, the ornaments all of copper. He staged for us also, for love of his art and of the work, my own plays, *The White Cockade*, *The Image*, *Dervorgilla*, and Mr. Yeats's *On Baile's Strand* with the great bronze gates used in other plays as well, in Lord Dunsany's *Glittering Gate* and in *The Countess Cathleen*. It was by him the scenery for Mr. Yeats's *Deirdre* was designed and painted, and for Synge's *Deirdre of the Sorrows*. I am proud to think how much "excellent beauty" he has brought to the help of our work.

CHAPTER IV

THE FIGHT OVER "THE PLAYBOY"

WHEN Synge's *Shadow of the Glen* was first played in the Molesworth Hall in 1903, some attacks were made on it by the *Sinn Fein* weekly newspaper. In the play the old husband pretends to be dead, the young wife listens to the offers of a young farmer, who asks her to marry him in the chapel of Rathvanna when "Himself will be quiet a while in the Seven Churches." The old man jumps up, drives her out of the house, refusing to make peace, and she goes away with a tramp, a stranger from the roads. Synge was accused of having borrowed the story from another country, from "a decadent Roman source," the story of the widow of Ephesus, and given it an Irish dress. He declared he had been told this story in the West of Ireland. It had already been given in Curtin's tales. Yet the same cry has been made from time to time. But it happened last winter I was at Newhaven, Massachusetts, with the Company, and we were asked to tea at the house of a Yale professor. There were a good many people there, and I had a few words with each, and as they spoke of the interest taken in the plays, a lady said: "My old nurse has been reading *The Shadow of the Glen*, but she says it is but a hearth tale; she had heard it long ago in Ireland." Then others came to talk to me, and next day I went on to speak at Smith College. It was not till later I remembered the refusal to take Synge's word, and that now *Shadow of the Glen* had been called a "hearth tale." I was sorry I had not asked for the old woman's words to be put down, but I could not remember among so many strangers who it was that had told me of them. But a little later, in New York, one of the younger Yale professors came round during the plays to the little sitting-room at the side of the stage at the Maxine Elliott Theatre where I received friends. I asked him to find out what I wanted to know, and after a while I was sent the words of the old woman, who is a nurse in a well-known philanthropic family: "Indeed, Miss, I 've heard that story many 's the time. It 's what in the old country we call a fireside story. In the evening the neighbours would be coming in and sitting about the big fire, in a great stone chimney like you know, and the big long hearthstone in front, and the men would be stretching out on their backs on the stones and telling stories just the like of that; how that an old man had a young wife, and he began to fear she was n't true to him, and he got himself into the bed and a big thorn stick with him, and made out to be dead, and when his wife was watching beside him in the night and thinking him safe dead, the other man came in and began talking to her to make her marry him; and himself jumped up out of the bed and gave them the great beating, just the same as in the book, Miss, only it reads more nice and refined like. Oh, there were many of those fireside stories they 'd tell!"

But the grumbling against this play was only in the papers and in letters, and it soon died out, although I find in a letter from Mr. Yeats before the opening of the Abbey: "The *Independent* has waked up and attacked us again with a note and a letter of a threatening nature warning us not to perform Synge again." The *Well of the Saints* was let pass without much comment, though we had very small audiences for it, for those were early days at the Abbey. It was another story when in 1907 *The Playboy of the Western World* was put on. There was a very large audience on the first night, a Saturday, January 26th. Synge was there, but Mr. Yeats was giving a lecture in Scotland. The first act got its applause and the second, though one felt the audience were a little puzzled, a little shocked at the wild language. Near the end of the third act there was some hissing. We had sent a telegram to Mr. Yeats after the first act—"Play great success"; but at the end we sent another—"Audience broke up in disorder at the word shift." For that plain English word was one of those objected to, and even the papers, in commenting, followed the example of some lady from the country, who wrote saying "the word omitted but understood was one she would blush to use even when she was alone."

On the Monday night *Riders to the Sea*, which was the first piece, went very well indeed. But in the interval after it, I noticed on one side of the pit a large group of men sitting together, not a woman among them. I told Synge I thought it a sign of some organised disturbance and he telephoned to have the police at hand. The first part of the first act went undisturbed. Then suddenly an uproar began. The group of men I had noticed booed, hooted, blew tin trumpets. The editor of one of the Dublin weekly papers was sitting next to me, and I asked him to count them. He did so and said there were forty making the disturbance. It was impossible to hear a word of the play. The curtain came down for a minute, but I went round and told the actors to go on playing to the end, even if not a word could be heard. The police, hearing the uproar, began to file in, but I thought the disturbers might tire themselves out if left alone, or be satisfied with having made their protest, and I asked them to go outside but stay within call in case of any attempt being made to injure the players or the stage. There were very few people in the stalls, but among them was Lord Walter Fitzgerald, grand-nephew of the patriot, the adored Lord Edward. He stood up and asked that he and others in the audience might be allowed to hear the play, but this leave was refused. The disturbance lasted to the end of the evening, not one word had been heard after the first ten minutes.

Next day Mr. Yeats arrived and took over the

management of affairs. Meanwhile I had asked a nephew at Trinity College to come and bring a few fellow athletes, that we might be sure of some ablebodied helpers in case of an attack on the stage. But, alas! the very sight of them was as a match to the resin of the pit, and a roar of defiance was flung back,—townsman against gownsman, hereditary enemies challenging each other as they are used to do when party or political processions march before the railings on College Green. But no iron railings divided pit and stalls, some scuffles added to the excitement, and it was one of our defenders at the last who was carried out bodily by the big actor who was playing Christy Mahon's slain father, and by Synge himself.

I had better help from another nephew. A caricature of the time shows him in evening dress with unruffled shirt cuffs, leading out disturbers of the peace. For Hugh Lane would never have worked the miracle of creating that wonderful gallery at sight of which Dublin is still rubbing its eyes, if he had not known that in matters of art the many count less than the few. I am not sure that in the building of our nation he may not have laid the most lasting stone; no fear of a charge of nepotism will scare me from "the noble pleasure of praising," and so I claim a place for his name above the thirty, among the chief, of our own mighty men.

There was a battle of a week. Every night protestors with their trumpets came and raised a din. Every night the police carried some of them off to the police courts. Every afternoon the papers gave reports of the trial before a magistrate who had not heard or read the play and who insisted on being given details of its incidents by the accused and by the police.

We held on, as we had determined, for the week during which we had announced the play would be acted. It was a definite fight for freedom from mob censorship. A part of the new National movement had been, and rightly, an attack on the stage Irishman, the vulgar and unnatural butt given on the English stage. We had the destroying of that scarecrow in mind among other things in setting up our Theatre. But the societies were impatient. They began to dictate here and there what should or should not be played. Mr. Colum's plays and Mr. Boyle's were found too harsh in their presentment of life. I see in a letter about a tour we were arranging: "Limerick has not yet come to terms. They have asked for copies of proposed plays that they may 'place same before the branch of the Gaelic League there.'"

At Liverpool a priest had arranged an entertainment. The audience did not like one of the plays and hooted. The priest thereupon appeared and apologised, saying he would take the play off. In Dublin, Mr. Martin Harvey, an old favourite, had been forced to take off after the first night a little play because its subject was Irish belief in witchcraft. The widow of a writer of Irish plays that had been fairly popular was picketed through Ireland with her company and was nearly ruined, no one being allowed to enter the doors. Finally, at, I think, Athlone, she was only allowed to produce a play after it had been cut and rearranged by a local committee, made up of the shopkeepers of the town. We would not submit Mr. Synge's work or any of the work we put on to such a test, nor would we allow any part of our audience to make itself final judge through preventing others from hearing and judging for themselves. We have been justified, for Synge's name has gone round the world, and we should have been ashamed for ever if we had not insisted on a hearing for his most important work. But, had it been a far inferior play and written by some young writer who had never been heard of, we should have had to do the same thing. If we had been obliged to give in to such organised dictation, we should of necessity have closed the Theatre. I respected the opinion of those among that group who were sincere. They, not used to works of imagination and wild fantasy, thought the play a libel on the Irish countryman, who has not put parricide upon his list of virtues; they thought the language too violent or it might be profane. The methods were another thing; when the tin trumpets were blown and brandished, we had to use the same loud methods and call in the police. We lost some of our audience by the fight; the pit was weak for a while, but one after another said, "There is no other theatre to go to," and came back. The stalls, curiously, who appeared to approve of our stand, were shy of us for a long time. They got an idea we were fond of noise and quarrels. That was our second battle, and even at the end of the week, we had won it.

#13

An organiser of agriculture, sent to County Clare, reported that the District Councils there were engaged in passing resolutions, "Against the French Government and *The Playboy*." Mrs. Coppinger in *The Image* says, on some such occasion, "Believe me there is not a Board or a Board Room west of the Shannon but will have a comrade cry put out between this and the Feast of Pentecost." And anyhow in our case some such thing happened.

But Synge's fantasy is better understood now even by those " who have never walked in Apollo's garden," and *The Playboy* holds its place in the repertory of the Abbey from year to year.

CHAPTER V

SYNGE

It is October now and leaves have fallen from the branches of the big copper-beech in the garden; I saw the stars shining through them last night. You were asleep then, but in the daytime you can see the sky all blue through their bareness. And the dry red heaps under them are noisy when pheasants, looking for mast, hurry away as you come calling, running, down the hill. The smooth trunk of the tree that was in shadow all through the summer time shines out now like silver. You stop to look at letters cut in the bark. You can read most of them yourself. You came under the wide boughs a few weeks ago, when a soldier who has gone now to set in order all the British dominions over sea, carved that "Ian H." far out of your reach, as high as his own high head. There is another name higher again, for the painter who cut that "A" and that "J" climbed up to write it again where we could not follow him, higher than the birds make their nests. There are letters of other names, "G. B. S." and "W. B. Y." Strangers know the names they stand for; they are easily known. But there to the north those letters, "J. M. S.," stand for a name that was not known at all at the time it was cut there, a few years before you were born.

The days are getting short and in the evening, when you ask me for something to paint or to scribble on, I sometimes give you one from a bundle of old sheets of paper, with three names printed at the head of it, with the picture of a woman and a dog. The names are those of three friends who worked together for a while: Yeats's name and my own and the name of John Millington Synge.

I first saw Synge in the north island of Aran. I was staying there, gathering folk-lore, talking to the people, and felt quite angry when I passed another outsider walking here and there, talking also to the people. I was jealous of not being alone on the island among the fishers and sea-weed gatherers. I did not speak to the stranger, nor was he inclined to speak to me. He also looked on

J. M. Synge

From a drawing by Robert Gregory in 1904

me as an intruder. I heard only his name. But a little later in the summer Mr. Yeats, who was staying with us at Coole, had a note from Synge, saying he was in Aran. They had met in Paris. Yeats wrote of him from there: "He is really a most excellent man. He lives in a little room which he has furnished himself; he is his own servant. He works very hard and is learning Breton; he will be a very useful scholar."

I asked him here and we became friends at once. I said of him in a letter: "One never has to rearrange one's mind to talk to him." He was quite direct, sincere, and simple, not only a good listener but too good a one, not speaking much in general society. His fellow guests at Coole always liked him, and he was pleasant and genial with them, though once, when he had come straight from life on a wild coast, he confessed that a somewhat warlike English lady in the house was "civilisation in its most violent form." There could be a sharp edge to his wit, as when he said that a certain actress (not Mrs. Campbell), whose modern methods he disliked, had turned Yeats' *Deirdre* into *The Second Mrs. Conchubar*. And once, when awakened from the anæsthetic after one of those hopeless operations, the first words that could be understood were, "Those damned English can't even swear without vulgarity."

He sent me later, when we had been long working at the Theatre, some reviews of his work from a German newspaper. "What gives me a sympathy with this new man is that he does not go off into sentimentality. Behind this legend I see a laughing face; then he raises his eyebrows in irony and laughs again. Herr Synge may not be a dramatist, he may not be a great poet, but he has something in him that I like, a thing that for many good Germans is a book with seven seals, that is, Humour." He writes a note with this, "I 'd like to quote about 'Humour,' but I don't want to tell Dublin I 'm maybe no dramatist; that would n't do."

Of his other side, Mr. J. B. Yeats wrote to me: "Coleridge said that all Shakespeare's characters from Macbeth to Dogberry are ideal realities, his comedies are poetry as an unlimited jest, and his tragedies 'poetry in deepest earnest.' Had he seen Synge's plays he would have called them, 'Poetry in unlimited sadness.'"

While with us, he hardly looked at a newspaper.

He seemed to look on politics and reforms with a sort of tolerant indifference, though he spoke once of something that had happened as "the greatest tragedy since Parnell's death." He told me that the people of the play he was writing often seemed the real people among whom he lived, and I think his dreamy look came from this. He spent a good deal of time wandering in our woods where many shy creatures still find their homes—marten cats and squirrels and otters and badgers,—and by the lake where wild swans come and go. He told Mr. Yeats he had given up wearing the black clothes he had worn for a while, when they were a fashion with writers, thinking they were not in harmony with nature, which is so sparing in the use of the harsh colour of the raven.

Simple things always pleased him. In his long illness in a Dublin hospital where I went to see him every day, he would ask for every detail of a search I was making for a couple of Irish terrier puppies to bring home, and laugh at my adventures again and again. And when I described to him the place where I had found the puppies at last, a little house in a suburb, with a long garden stretching into wide fields, with a view of the hills beyond, he was excited and said that it was just such a Dublin home as he wanted, and as he had been sure was somewhere to be found. He asked me at this time about a village on the Atlantic coast, where I had stayed for a while, over a post-office, and where he hoped he might go for his convalescence instead of to Germany, as had been arranged for him. I said, in talking, that I felt more and more the time wasted that was not spent in Ireland, and he said: "That is just my feeling."

The rich, abundant speech of the people was a delight to him. When my *Cuchulain of Muirthemme* came out, he said to Mr. Yeats he had been amazed to find in it the dialect he had been trying to master. He wrote to me: "Your *Cuchulain* is a part of my daily bread." I say this with a little pride, for I was the first to use the Irish idiom as it is spoken, with intention and with belief in it. Dr. Hyde indeed has used it with fine effect in his *Love Songs of Connacht*, but alas! gave it up afterwards, in deference to some Dublin editor. He wrote to me after his first visit: "I had a very prosperous journey up from Gort. At Athenry an old Irish-speaking wanderer made my acquaintance. He claimed to be the best singer in England, Ireland, and America. One night, he says, he sang a song at Moate, and a friend of his heard the words in Athenry. He was so much struck by the event, he had himself examined by one who knew, and found that his singing did not come out of his lungs but out of his heart, which is a 'winged heart'!"

At the time of his first visit to Coole he had written some poems, not very good for the most part, and a play, which was not good at all. I read it again after his death when, according to his written wish, helping Mr. Yeats in sorting out the work to be published or set aside, and again it seemed but of slight merit. But a year later he brought us his two plays, *The Shadow of the Glen*, and the *Riders to the Sea*, both masterpieces, both perfect in their way. He had got emotion, the driving force he needed, from his life among the people, and it was the working in dialect that had set free his style.

He was anxious to publish his book on Aran and these two plays, and so have something to add to that "£40 a year and a new suit when I am too shabby," he used with a laugh to put down as his income. He wrote to me from Paris in February,

1902: "I don't know what part of Europe you may be in now, but I suppose this will reach you if I send it to Coole. I want to tell you the evil fate of my Aran book and ask your advice. It has been to two London publishers, one of whom was sympathetic, though he refused it, as he said it would not be a commercial success, and the other inclined to be scornful.

"Now that you have seen the book, do you think that there would be any chance of Mr. N— taking it up? I am afraid he is my only chance, but I don't know whether there is any possibility of getting him to bring out a book of the kind at his own expense, as after all there is very little folk-lore in it."

I took the book to London and had it retyped, for Synge, as I myself do, typed his own manuscripts, and the present one was very faint and rubbed. Both Mr. Yeats and I took it to publishers, but they would not accept it. Synge writes in March, 1903:

"My play came back from the *Fortnightly* as not suitable for their purpose. I don't think that Mr. J— intends to bring out the Aran book. I saw him on my way home, but he seemed hopelessly undecided, saying one minute he liked it very much, and that it might be a great success, and that he wanted to be in touch with the Irish movement, and then going off in the other direction, and fearing that it might fall perfectly flat! Finally he asked me to let him consider it a little longer!"

I was no more successful. I wrote to Mr. Yeats, who was in America: "I went to Mr. B. about the music for your book. . . I think I told you he had never opened the Synge MS., and said he would rather have nothing to do with it. Masefield has it now."

Then I had a note: "Dear Lady Gregory, I saw Mr. N. yesterday and spoke to him about Synge's new play [*Riders to the Sea*], which struck me as being in some ways better even than the other. He has promised to read it if it is sent to him, though he does not much care for plays. Will you post it to, the Editor, *Monthly Review*. . . . Yours very truly, Arthur Symons."

Nothing came of that and in December Synge writes:

"I am delighted to find that there is a prospect of getting the book out at last, and equally grateful for the trouble you have taken with it. I am writing to Masefield to-day to thank him and ask him by all means to get Matthews to do as he proposes. Do you think if he brings out the book in the spring, I should add the *Tinkers?* I was getting on well with the blind people (in *Well of the Saints*), till about a month ago when I suddenly got ill with influenza and a nasty attack on my lung. I am getting better now, but I cannot work yet satisfactorily, so I hardly know when the play is likely to be finished. There is no use trying to hurry on with a thing of that sort when one is not in the mood."

Yet, after all, the Aran book was not published till 1907, when Synge's name had already gone up. *The Shadow of the Glen* and *Riders to the Sea* were published by Mr. Elkin Matthews in 1905. *Riders to the Sea* had already been published in *Samhain*, the little annual of our Theatre, edited by Mr. Yeats. And in America a friend of ours and of the Theatre had printed some of the plays in a little edition of fifty copies, thus saving his copyright. It was of Synge and of others as well as myself I thought when, in dedicating a book to John Quinn during my first winter in America,

I wrote, "best friend, best helper, these half score years on this side of the sea."

When Synge had joined us in the management of the Theatre, he took his share of the work, and though we were all amateurs then, we got on somehow or other. He writes about a secretary we had sent for him to report on: "He seems very willing and I think he may do very well if he does not take fright at us. He still thinks it was a terrible thing for Yeats to suggest that Irish people should sell their souls and for you to put His Sacred Majesty James II. into a barrel. He should be very useful in working up an audience; an important part of our work that we have rather neglected. By the way, the annual meeting of our company must be held, I suppose, before the year is up. It would be well to have it before we pay off Ryan, as otherwise we shall all be sitting about, looking with curiosity and awe at the balance sheet."

He went on bravely with his work, but always fighting against ill health. He writes: "Feb. 15, '06. Many thanks for the MS. of *Le Médecin*. I think he is entirely admirable and is certain to go well. This is just a line to acknowledge

9

the MS., as I suppose I shall see you in a day or two.

"My play has made practically no headway since, as I have been down for ten days with bronchitis. My lung is not touched, however, and I have got off well considering. I hope I shall be all right by next week."

[About the same date.]: "I am pleased with the way my play is going, but I find it is quite impossible to rush through with it now, so I rather think I shall take it and the typewriter to some place in Kerry where I could work. By doing so, I will get some sort of holiday and still avoid dropping the play again, which is a rather dangerous process. If I do this, I will be beyond posts. . . . If I do not get a good summer, I generally pay for it in the winter in extra bouts of influenza and all its miseries."

"August 12, '06. I shall be very glad, thanks, to go down and read you my play (*The Playboy*), if it is finished in time, but there is still a great deal to do. I have had a very steady week's work since last Sunday and have made good way, but my head is getting very tired. Working in hot weather takes a lot out of me."

"November 25, '06. I have had rather a worse attack than I expected when I wrote my last note, but I am much better now, and out as usual. One of my lungs, however, has been a little touched, so I shall have to be careful for a while. Would it be possible to put off *The Playboy* for a couple of weeks? I am afraid if I went to work at him again now, and then rehearsed all December, I would be very likely to knock up badly before I was done with him. My doctor says I may do so if it is *necessary*, but he advises me to take a couple of weeks' rest if it can be managed. That cousin of mine who etches is over here now, and he wants me to stay with him for a fortnight in a sort of country house he has in Surrey; so if you think *The Playboy* can be put off, I will go across on Thursday or Friday and get back in time to see *The Shadowy Waters* and get *The Playboy* under way for January. What do you think? If so, I would like to read the third act of *Playboy* to you before I go, and then make final changes while I am away, as I shall have a quiet time."

He worked very hard at *The Playboy*, altering it a good deal as he went on. He had first planned the opening act in the ploughed field, where the quarrel between Christy and his father took place. But when he thought of the actual stage, he could not see any possible side wings for that "wide, windy corner of high distant hills." He had also thought that the scene of the return of the father should be at the very door of the chapel where Christy was to wed Pegeen. But in the end all took place within the one cottage room. We all tried at that time to write our plays so as to require as little scene-shifting as possible for the sake of economy of scenery and of stage hands.

In October, 1906, Synge wrote to Mr. Yeats: "My play, though in its last agony, is not finished, and I cannot promise it for any definite day. It is more than likely that when I read it to you and Fay, there will be little things to alter that have escaped me, and with my stuff it takes time to get even half a page of new dialogue fully into key with what goes before it. The play, I think, will be one of the longest we have done, and in places extremely difficult. If we said the 19th, I could only have six or seven full rehearsals, which would not, I am quite sure, be enough. I am very sorry, but what is to be done?"

Then he wrote to me in November: "May I

read *The Playboy* to you and Yeats and Fay, some time to-morrow, Saturday, or Monday, according as it suits you all? A little verbal correction is still necessary, and one or two structural points may need—I fancy do need—revision, but I would like to have your opinions on it before I go any further."

I remember his bringing the play to us in Dublin, but he was too hoarse to read it, and it was read by Mr. Fay. We were almost bewildered by its abundance and fantasy, but we felt, and Mr. Yeats said very plainly, that there was far too much "bad language." There were too many violent oaths, and the play itself was marred by this. I did not think it was fit to be put on the stage without cutting. It was agreed that it should be cut in rehearsal. A fortnight before its production, Mr. Yeats, thinking I had seen a rehearsal, wrote: "I would like to know how you thought *The Playboy* acted. . . . Have they cleared many of the objectionable sentences out of it?" I did not, however, see a rehearsal and did not hear the play again until the night of its production, and then I told Synge that the cuts were not enough, that many more should be made. He gave me leave to do this, and, in consultation with the players, I took out many phrases which, though in the printed book, have never since that first production been spoken on our stage. I am sorry they were not taken out before it had been played at all, but that is just what happened.

On Saturday, January 26, 1907, I found a note from Synge on my arrival in Dublin: "I do not know how things will go to-night. The day company are all very steady but some of the outsiders in a most deplorable state of uncertainty. . . . I have a sort of second edition of influenza and I am looking gloomily at everything. Fay has worked very hard all through, and everything has gone smoothly."

I think the week's rioting helped to break down his health. He was always nervous at a first production and the unusual excitement attending this one upset him. He took a chill and was kept to his bed for a while. Yet he got away to wild places while he could. He wrote to me from the Kerry coast: "My journey went off all right, and though I had a terribly wet night in Tralee, I was able to ride on here next day. When I came up to the house, I found to my horror a large green tent pitched in the haggard and thought I had run my head into a Gaelic League settlement at last. However, it turned out to be only a band of sappers, who have since moved on." And again: "The day after to-morrow I move on, bag and baggage, to the Great Blasket Island. It is probably even more primitive than Aran, and I am wild with joy at the prospect. I will tell you of my new abode. I am to go out in a curragh on Sunday, when the people are going back from Mass on the mainland, and I am to lodge with the King!"

It was only in the country places he was shy of the Gaelic League. In August, 1906, he says: "I went to the Oireactas on Thursday to see their plays. Their propagandist play, done by the Ballaghadereen company, was clever, with some excellent dialogue. The peasants who acted it were quite admirable. I felt really enthusiastic about the whole show, although the definitely propagandist fragments were, of course, very crude. The play was called, I think, *an T-Atruighe mor* (The big change). I think I have spelled it wrong. It would probably read badly."

The last year was still a struggle against failing

strength: "April, '08. I have been waiting from day to day to write, so that I might say something definite about my 'tin-tacks' (an allusion to the old man in *Workhouse Ward* who had pains like tin-tacks in his inside) and possible plans. I was with the doctor again to-day, and he thinks I may have to go into hospital again and perhaps have an operation, but things are uncertain for a day or two . . . . I fear there is little possibility of my being able to go to the shows this week, so I do not know if you ought to come up, if you can without inconvenience. I am rather afraid of slovenly shows if there are poor houses and no one there to supervise. It is very trying having to drop my rehearsals of *Well of the Saints*. In fact, this unlooked for complication is a terrible upset everyway—I have so much to do."

"August 28, '08. I have just been with Sir C. Ball. He seems to think I am going on very well, and says I may ride and bicycle and do what I like! All the same I am not good for much yet. I get tired out very easily. I am half inclined to go to the British Association matinée on Friday. I would like to hear Yeats' speech, and I don't think it would do me any harm. In any case, I will go in and see you when you are up. I think of going away to Germany or somewhere before very long. I am not quite well enough for the West of Ireland in this broken weather, and I think the complete change would do me most good. I have old friends on the Rhine I could stay with, if I decide to go there. I hear great accounts of the Abbey this week. It almost looks as if Dublin was beginning to know we are there. I have been fiddling with my *Deirdre* a little. I think I 'll have to cut it down to two longish acts. The middle act in Scotland is impossible. . . . They have been playing *The Well of the Saints* in Munich. I have just got £3:10, royalties. It was a one-act version I have just heard this minute, compressed from my text!"

"January 3, '09. I have done a great deal to *Deirdre* since I saw you, chiefly in the way of strengthening motives and recasting the general scenario; but there is still a good deal to be done with the dialogue and some scenes in the first act must be rewritten to make them fit in with the new parts I have added. I only work a little every day, and I suffer more than I like with indigestion and general uneasiness inside. . . . The doctors are vague and don't say much that is definite. . . .

"They are working at the *Miser* now and are all very pleased with it and with themselves, as I hear. I have not been in to see a rehearsal yet, as I keep out in the country as much as I can."

But his strength did not last long enough to enable him to finish *Deirdre of the Sorrows*, his last play. After he was gone, we did our best to bring the versions together, and we produced it early in the next year, but it needed the writer's hand. I did my best for it, working at its production through snowy days and into winter nights until rheumatism seized me with a grip I have never shaken off. I wrote to Mr. Yeats: "I still hope we can start with *Deirdre*. I will be in Dublin for rehearsals in Christmas week, though I still hope to get to Paris for Christmas with Robert, but it may not be worth while. I will spend all January at the Theatre, but I must be back on the first of February to do some planting that cannot be put off." And again: "I am more hopeful of *Deirdre* now. I have got Conchubar and Fergus off at the last in Deirdre's long speech and that makes an immense improvement. She looks lonely and pathetic with the other two women crouching and rocking themselves on the floor."

For we have done our best for Synge's work since we lost him, as we did while he was with us here.

He had written a poem which was in the Press at the time of his death:

"With Fifteen-ninety or Sixteen-sixteen
We end Cervantes, Marot, Nashe or Green;
Then Sixteen-thirteen till two score and nine
Is Crashaw's niche, that honey-lipped divine.
And so when all my little work is done
They 'll say I came in Eighteen-seventy-one,
And died in Dublin. What year will they write
For my poor passage to the stall of Night?"

Early in 1909 he was sent again into a private hospital in Dublin. A letter came to me from Mr. Yeats, dated March 24th: "In the early morning Synge said to the nurse 'It's no use fighting death any longer,' and turned over and died."

CHAPTER VI

THE FIGHT WITH THE CASTLE

IN the summer of 1909 I went one day from London to Ayot St. Lawrence, a Hertfordshire village, to consult Mr. Bernard Shaw on some matters connected with our Theatre. When I was leaving, he gave me a little book, *The Shewing up of Blanco Posnet*, which had just been printed, although not published. It had, however, been already rejected by the Censor, as all readers of the newspapers know; and from that quiet cottage the fiery challenge-giving answers had been sent out. I read the play as I went back in the train, and when at St. Pancras Mr. Yeats met me to talk over the business that had taken me away, I showed him the little book that had been given its black ball, and I said, "Hypocrites."

A little time afterwards Mr. Shaw offered us the play for the Abbey, for the Censor has no jurisdiction in Ireland—an accidental freedom. We accepted it and put it in rehearsal that we might produce it in Horse Show week. We were without a regular stage manager at that time, and thought to have it produced by one of the members of the Company. But very soon the player who had taken it in charge found the work too heavy and troublesome, and withdrew from the stage management, though not from taking a part. I had a letter one morning telling me this, and I left by the next train for Dublin. As I left, I sent a wire to a London actor—a friend—asking if he could come over and help us out of this knot. Meanwhile, that evening, and before his answer came, I held a rehearsal, the first I had ever taken quite alone. I thought out positions during the night, and next morning, when I had another rehearsal, I began to find an extraordinary interest and excitement in the work. I saw that Blanco's sermon, coming as it did after bustling action, was in danger of seeming monotonous. I broke it up by making him deliver the first part standing up on the Sheriff's bench, then bringing him down to sit on the table and speak some of the words into the face of Elder Posnet. After that I sent him with a leap on to the table for the last phrases. I was very much pleased with the effect of this action, and by the time a telegram told me my London friend could come, I was confident enough to do without him. We were very proud and pleased when the whole production was taken to London later by the Stage Society. I have produced plays since then, my own and a few others. It is tiring work; one spends so much of one's own vitality.

That is what took me away from home to Dublin in that summer time, when cities are out of season. Mr. Yeats had stayed on at Coole at his work, and my letters to him, and letters after that to my son and to Mr. Shaw, will tell what happened through those hot days, and of the battle with Dublin Castle, which had taken upon itself to make the writ of the London Censor run at the Abbey.

I received while in Dublin, the following letter from a permanent official in Dublin Castle:

"Dear Lady Gregory:

"I am directed by the Lord Lieutenant to state that His Excellency's attention has been called to an announcement in the Public Press that a play entitled *The Shewing up of Blanco Posnet* is about to be performed in the Abbey Theatre.

"This play was written for production in a London theatre, and its performance was disallowed by the Authority which in England is charged with the Censorship of stage plays. The play does not deal with an Irish subject, and it is not an Irish play in any other sense than that its author was born in Ireland. It is now proposed to produce this play in the Abbey Theatre, which was founded for the express purpose of encouraging dramatic art in Ireland, and of fostering a dramatic school growing out of the life of the country.

"The play in question does not seem well adapted to promote these laudable objects or to belong to the class of plays originally intended to be performed in the Abbey Theatre, as described in the evidence on the hearing of the application for the Patent.

"However this may be, the fact of the proposed performance having been brought to the notice of the Lord Lieutenant, His Excellency cannot evade the responsibility cast upon him of considering whether the play conforms in other respects to the conditions of the Patent.

"His Excellency, after the most careful consideration, has arrived at the conclusion that in its original form the play is not in accordance either with the assurances given by those interested when the Patent was applied for, or with the conditions and restrictions contained in the Patent as granted by the Crown.

"As you are the holder of the Patent in trust for the generous founder of the Theatre, His Excellency feels bound to call your attention, and also the attention of those with whom you are associated, to the terms of the Patent and to the serious consequences which the production of the play in its original form might entail. . ."

I tell what followed in letters written to Coole:

"Thursday, August 12th. At the Theatre this morning the Secretary told me Whitney & Moore (our solicitors) had telephoned that they had a hint there would be interference with the production of *Blanco Posnet* by the Castle, and would like to see me.

"I went to see Dr. Moore. He said a Castle Official, whose name he would not give, had called the day before yesterday and said, 'As a friend of Sir Benjamin Whitney, I have come to tell you that if this play is produced it will be a very expensive thing for Miss Horniman.' Dr. Moore took this to mean the Patent would be forfeited. I talked the matter over with him and asked if he would get further information from his friend as to what method they meant to adopt, for I would not risk the immediate forfeiture of the Patent, but would not mind a threat of refusal to give a new Patent, as by that time—1910—perhaps neither the present Lord Lieutenant nor the present Censor would be in office.

"Dr. Moore said he would go and see his friend, and at a quarter past two I had a message on the telephone from him that I had better see the Castle Official or that he wished to see me (I did n't hear very well) before 3 o'clock. I went to the Castle and saw the Official. He said, 'Well.' I said, 'Are you going to cut off our heads?' He said, 'This is a very serious business; I think you are very ill-advised to think of putting on this play. May I ask how it came about?' I said, 'Mr. Shaw offered it and we accepted it.' He said, 'You have put us in a most difficult and disagreeable position by putting on a play to which the English Censor objected.' I answered, 'We do not take his view of it, and we think it hypocrisy objecting to a fallen woman in homespun on the stage, when a fallen woman in satin has been the theme of such a great number of plays that have been passed.' He said, 'It is not that the Censor objected to; it is the use of certain expressions which may be considered blasphemous. Could not they be left out?' 'Then there would be no play. The subject of the play is a man, a horse-thief, shaking his fist at Heaven, and finding afterwards that Heaven is too strong for him. If there were no defiance, there could be no victory. It is the same theme that Milton has taken in Satan's defiance in *Paradise Lost*. I consider it a deeply religious play, and one that could hurt no man, woman, or child. If it had been written by some religious leader, or even by a dramatist considered "safe," nonconformists would admire and approve of it.' He said, 'We have nothing to do with that, the fact for us is that the Censor has banned it.' I said, 'Yes, and passed *The Merry Widow*, which is to be performed here the same week, and which I have heard is objectionable, and *The Devil*, which I saw in London.' He said, 'We would not have interfered, but what can we do when we see such paragraphs as these?' handing me a cutting from the *Irish Times* headed, 'Have we a Censor?' I replied, 'We have not written or authorised it, as you might see by its being incorrect. I am sole Patentee of the Theatre.' He said, 'Dublin society will call out against us if we let it go on.' 'Lord Iveagh has taken six places.' 'For that play?' 'Yes, for that play, and I believe Dublin society is likely to follow Lord Iveagh.' He went on, 'And Archbishop Walsh may object.' I was silent. He said, 'It is very hard on the Lord Lieutenant. You should have had more consideration for him.' I replied, 'We did not know or remember that the power rested with him, but it *is* hard on him, for he can't please everybody.' He said, 'Will you not give it up?' 'What will you do if we go on? 'Either take no notice or take the Patent from you at once.' I said, 'If you decide to forfeit our Patent, we will not give a public performance; but if we give no performance to be judged by, we shall rest under the slur of having tried to produce something bad and injurious.' 'We must not provoke Public opinion.' 'We provoked Nationalist public opinion in *The*

Playboy, and you did not interfere.' 'Aye,' said he, 'exactly so, that was quite different; that had not been banned by the Censor.' I said, 'Time has justified us, for we have since produced *The Playboy* in Dublin and on tour with success, and it will justify us in the case of this play.' 'But *Blanco Posnet* is very inferior to *The Playboy*.' I said, 'Even so, Bernard Shaw has an intellectual position above that of Mr. Synge, though he is not above him in imaginative power. He is recognised as an intellectual force, and his work cannot be despised.' 'Lord Aberdeen will have to decide.' 'I should like him to know,' I said, 'that from a business point of view the refusal to allow this play, already announced, to be given would do us a serious injury.' He said, 'No advertisements have been published.' 'Yes,' I said, 'the posters have been out some days, and there is a good deal of booking already from England as well as here. We are just beginning to pay our way as a Theatre. We should be able to do so if we got about a dozen more stalls regularly. The people who would take stalls will be frightened off by your action. The continuance of our Theatre at all may depend on what you do now. We are giving a great deal of employment, spending in Dublin over £1500 a year, and our Company bears the highest possible character.' He said, 'I know that well.' I said, 'I know Lord Aberdeen is friendly to our Theatre, though he does not come to it, not liking the colour of our carpets.' He said 'He is a supporter of the drama. He was one of Sir Henry Irving's pall-bearers.' 'When shall we know the decision?' 'In a day or two, perhaps to-morrow. You can produce it in Cork, Galway, or Waterford. It is only in Dublin the Lord Lieutenant has power.' He read from time to time a few lines from the Patent or Act of Parliament before him, 'just to get them into your head.' The last words he read were, 'There must be no profane representation of sacred personages'; 'and that,' he said, 'applies to Blanco Posnet's representations of the Deity.' I told him of the Censor's note on *The Playboy*, 'The expression "Khaki cut-throats" must be cut out, together with any others that may be considered derogatory to His Majesty's Forces,' and he laughed. Then I said, 'How can we think much of the opinion of a man like that?' He said, 'I believe he was a bank manager.' We then said good-bye."

"Friday, 5 o'c. Dr. Moore sent for me at 4 o'clock. I went with W. B. Yeats, who had arrived. The Crown Solicitor at the Castle, Sir B. Whitney's 'friend,' had called and told him the Lord Lieutenant was 'entirely opposed to the play being proceeded with and would use every power the law gave him to stop it,' and that, 'it would be much better for us to lay the play aside.'

"We decided to go on with the performance and let the Patent be forfeited, and if we must die, die gloriously. Yeats was for this course, and I agreed. Then I thought it right to let the Permanent Official know my change of intention, and, after some unsuccessful attempts on the telephone, W. B. Y. and I went to see him at the Castle. He was very smiling and amiable this time, and implored us, as we had understood him to do through the telephone, to save the Lord Lieutenant from his delicate position. 'You defy us, you advertise it under our very nose, at the time everyone is making a fight with the Censor.' He threatened to take away our Patent before the play came on at all, if we persisted in the intention. I said that would give us a fine case. Yeats said we intended to do *Œdipus*, that this also was a censored play, although so unobjectionable to religious minds that it had been performed in the Catholic University of Nôtre Dame, and that we should be prevented if we announced it now. He replied, 'Leave that till the time comes, and you need n't draw our attention to it.' We said the *Irish Times* might again draw his attention to it. He proposed our having a private performance only. I said, 'I had a letter from Mr. Shaw objecting to that course.' He moaned, and said, 'It is very hard upon us. Can you suggest no way out of it?' We answered, 'None, except our being left alone.' 'Oh, Lady Gregory,' he said, 'appeal to your own common sense.' When I mentioned Shaw's letter, he said, 'All Shaw wants is to use the Lord Lieutenant as a whip to lay upon the Censor.' Yeats said, 'Shaw would use him in that way whatever happens.' 'I know he will,' said the Official. At last he asked if we could get Mr. Shaw to take out the passages he had already offered to take out for the Censor. We agreed to ask him to do this, as we felt the Castle was beaten, as the play even then would still be the one forbidden in England."

This is the letter I had received from Mr. Shaw:

"10 Adelphi Terrace, W. C. 12th August, 1909. Your news is almost too good to be true. If the Lord Lieutenant would only forbid an Irish play without reading it, and after it had been declared entirely guiltless and admirable by the leading high class journal on the side of his own party [*The Nation*], forbid it at the command of an official of the King's household in London, then the green flag would indeed wave over Abbey Street, and we should have questions in Parliament and all manner of reverberating advertisement and nationalist sympathy for the Theatre.

"I gather from your second telegram that the play has, perhaps, been submitted for approval. If so, that will be the worse for us, as the Castle can then say they forbade it on its demerits without the slightest reference to the Lord Chamberlain.

"In any case, do not threaten them with a contraband performance. Threaten that we shall be suppressed; that we shall be made martyrs of; that we shall suffer as much and as publicly as possible. Tell them that they can depend on me to burn with a brighter blaze and louder yells than all Foxe's martyrs."

Mr. Shaw telegraphed his answer to the demand for cuts:

"The *Nation* article gives particulars of cuts demanded, which I refused as they would have destroyed the religious significance of the play. The line about moral relations is dispensable as they are mentioned in several other places; so it can be cut if the Castle is silly enough to object to such relations being called immoral, but I will cut nothing else. It is an insult to the Lord Lieutenant to ignore him and refer me to the requirements of a subordinate English Official. I will be no party to any such indelicacy. Please say I said so, if necessary."

I give in the Appendix the *Nation* article to which he refers. My next letter home says: "August 14. Having received the telegram from Shaw and the *Nation* article, we went to the Castle to see the Official, but only found his secretary, who offered to speak to him through a telephone, but the telephone was wheezy, and after long trying, all we could arrive at was that he wanted to know if we had seen Sir H. Beerbohm Tree's evidence, in which he said there were passages in *Blanco* that would be better out. Then he proposed our going to see him at his house, as he has gout and rheumatism and could n't come to us.

"We drove to his house. He began on Tree, but Yeats told him Tree was the chief representative of the commercial theatre we are opposed to. He then proposed our giving a private performance, and we again told him Shaw had forbidden that. I read him the telegram refusing cuts, but he seemed to have forgotten that he had asked for cuts, and repeated his appeal to spare the Lord Lieutenant. I showed him the *Nation* article, and he read it and said 'But the *Book of Job* is not by the same author as *Blanco Posnet.*' Yeats said, 'Then if you could, you would censor the Deity?' 'Just so,' said he. He asked if we could make no concession. We said, 'no,' but that if they decided to take away the Patent, we should put off the production till the beginning of our season, end of September, and produce it with *Œdipus;* then they would have to suppress both together. He brightened up and said, if we could put it off, things would be much easier, as the Commission would not be sitting then or the Public be so much interested in the question. I said 'Of course we should have to announce at once that it was in consequence of the threatened action of the Castle we had postponed it.' 'Oh, you really don't mean that! You would let all the bulls loose. It would be much better not to say anything at all, or to say the rehearsals took longer than you expected.' 'The public announcement will be more to our own advantage.' 'Oh, that is dreadful!' I said, 'We did not give in one quarter of an inch to Nationalist Ireland at *The Playboy* time, and we certainly cannot give in one quarter of an inch to the Castle.'

"'We must think of Archbishop Walsh!' I said, 'The Archbishop would be slow to move, for if he orders his flock to keep away from our play, he can't let them attend many of the Censor's plays, and the same thing applies to the Lord Lieutenant.' The Official said, 'I know that.' We said 'We did not give in to the Church when Cardinal Logue denounced the *Countess Cathleen*. We played it under police protection.' 'I never heard of that. Why did he object?' Yeats said, 'For exactly the same objection as is made to the present one, speeches made by demons in the play.'

"Yeats spoke very seriously then about the principle involved; pointing out that we were trying to create a model on which a great national theatre may be founded in the future, that if we accepted the English Censor's ruling in Ireland, he might forbid a play like Wills' *Robert Emmet*, which Irving was about to act, and was made to give up for political reasons. He said, 'You want, in fact, to have liberty to produce all plays refused by the Censor.' I said, 'We have produced none in the past and not only that, we have refused plays that we thought would hurt Catholic religious feeling. We refused, for instance, to produce Synge's *Tinker's Wedding*, much as we uphold his work, because a drunken priest made ridiculous appears in it. That very play was directly after Synge's death asked for by Tree, whom you have been holding up to us, for production in London.' He said, 'I am very sorry attention was drawn to the play. If no attention had been drawn to it by the papers, we should be all right. It is so wrong to produce it while the Commission is actually sitting and the whole question *sub judice*. We are in close official relation with the English officials of whom the Lord Chamberlain is one; that is the whole question.' We said, 'We see no way out of it. We are determined to produce the play. We cannot accept the Censor's decision as applying to Ireland and you must make up your mind what course to take, but we ask to be let known as soon as possible because if we are to be suppressed, we must find places for our players, who will be thrown out of work.' He threw up his hands and exclaimed, 'Oh, my dear lady, but do not speak of such a thing as possible!' 'Why,' I asked, 'what else have you been threatening all the time?' He said, 'Well, the Lord Lieutenant will be here on Tuesday and will decide. He has not given his attention to the matter up to this' (this does not bear out the Crown Solicitor's story); 'Perhaps you had better stay to see him.' I told him that I wanted to get home, but would stay if absolutely necessary. He said, 'Oh, yes, stay and you will probably see Lady Aberdeen also.' "

Mr. Shaw's next letter was from Kerry where he

was motoring. In it he said: "I saw an *Irish Times* to-day with *Blanco* announced for production; so I presume the Castle has not put its foot down. The officials made an appalling technical blunder in acting as agents of the Lord Chamberlain in Ireland; and I worded my telegram in such a way as to make it clear that I knew the value of that indiscretion.

"I daresay the telegram reached the Castle before it reached you."

Meanwhile on August 15th I had written to the Castle:

"I am obliged to go home to-morrow, so if you have any news for us, will you very kindly let us have it at Coole.

"We are, as you know, arranging to produce *Blanco* on Wednesday, 25th, as advertised and booked for, unless you serve us with a 'Threatening notice,' in which case we shall probably postpone it till September 30th and produce it with the already promised *Œdipus*.

"I am very sorry to have given you so much trouble and worry, and, as we told you, we had no idea the responsibility would fall on any shoulders but our own; but I think we have fully explained to you the reasons that make it necessary for us now to carry the matter through."

I received the following answer:

"I am sorry you have been obliged to return to Galway. His Excellency, who arrived this morning, regrets that he has missed the opportunity of seeing you and desires me to say that if you wished an interview with him on Thursday, he would be glad to receive you at the Viceregal Lodge.

"He will give the subject which has been discussed between us his earliest attention."

I received by the same post a long and very kind letter from the Lord Lieutenant, written with his own hand. I am sorry that it was marked "Private," and so I cannot give it here. I may, however, quote the words that brought us back to Dublin. "It would seem that some further personal conference might be very desirable and therefore I hope that it may be possible for you to revisit Dublin on the earliest available day. I shall, of course, be most happy to have an opportunity for a talk with Mr. Yeats."

So my next letter home says: "Friday, 20th. We arrived at the Broadstone yesterday at 2.15, and were met by the Official's secretary, who asked us to go to the Viceregal Lodge. Arrived there, another secretary came and asked me to go and see the Lord Lieutenant alone, saying Mr. Yeats could go in later."

Alas! I must be discreet and that conversation with the King's representative must not be given to the world, at least by me. I can only mention external things: Mr. Yeats, until he joined the conference, being kept by the secretary, whether from poetical or political reasons, to the non-committal subject of Spring flowers; my grieved but necessary contumacy; our joint and immovable contumacy; the courtesy shown to us and, I think, also by us; the kindly offers of a cup of tea; the consuming desire for that tea after the dust of the railway journey all across Ireland; our heroic refusal, lest its acceptance should in any way, even if it did not weaken our resolve, compromise our principles. . . . His Excellency's gracious nature has kept no malice and he has since then publicly taken occasion to show friendship for our Theatre. I felt it was a business forced upon him, who had used his high office above all for reconcilement, as it was upon me, who had lived under a peaceful star for some half a hundred years. I think it was a relief to both of us when at last he asked us to go on to the Castle and see again "a very experienced Official."

I may now quote again from my letters: "We found the Official rather in a temper. He had been trying to hear Lord Aberdeen's account of the interview through the telephone and could not. We gave our account, he rather threatening in tone, repeating a good deal of what he had said before. He said we should be as much attacked as they, whatever happened, and that men connected with two newspapers had told him they were only waiting for an opportunity of attacking not only the Lord Lieutenant but the Abbey, if the play is allowed; so we should also catch it. I said, '*Après vous.*' He said Mr. Yeats had stated in the Patent Enquiry, the Abbey was for the production of romantic work. I quoted Parnell, 'Who shall set bounds to the march of a Nation?' We told him our Secretary had reported, 'Very heavy booking, first class people, *a great many from the Castle.*'

"He said he would see the Lord Lieutenant on his way home. We went to Dame Street Post Office and wired to Mr. Shaw: 'Have seen Viceroy.

Deleted immoral relations, refused other cuts. He is writing to King, who supports Censor."

Then, as holder of the Patent, I took counsel's opinion on certain legal points, of which the most vital was this:

"Should counsel be of opinion that the Crown will serve notice requiring the play to be discontinued, then counsel will please say what penalty he thinks querist would expose herself to by disregarding the notice of the Crown and continuing the representation?"

The answer to this question was:

"If the theatre ceases to be licensed, as pointed out above, and any performance for gain takes place there, the penalty under the 26. Geo. III. cap 57, sec. (2) *is £300 for each offence*, to be recovered in a '*qui tam*' action; one half of the £300 going to the Rotunda Hospital, the other half to the informer who sues."

Mr. Yeats and I were just going to a rehearsal at the Abbey on the evening of August 21st when we received a letter from the Castle, telling us that a formal legal document, forbidding the performance of the play, would reach us immediately. The matter had now become a very grave one. We knew that we should, if we went on and this threat were carried out, lose not only the Patent but that the few hundred pounds that we had been able to save and with which we could have supported our players till they found other work, would be forfeited. This thought of the players made us waver, and very sadly we agreed that we must give up the fight. We did not say a word of this at the Abbey but went on rehearsing as usual. When we had left the Theatre and were walking through the lamp-lighted streets, we found that during those two or three hours our minds had come to the same decision, that we had given our word, that at all risks we must keep it or it would never be trusted again; that we must in no case go back, but must go on at any cost.

We wrote a statement in which we told of the pressure put upon us and the objections made, but of these last we said: "there is nothing to change our conviction that so far from containing offence for any sincere and honest mind, Mr. Shaw's play is a high and weighty argument upon the working of the Spirit of God in man's heart, or to show that it is not a befitting thing for us to set upon our stage the work of an Irishman, who is also the most famous of living dramatists, after that work has been silenced in London by what we believe an unjust decision.

"One thing" we continued, "is plain enough, an issue that swallows up all else and makes the merit of Mr. Shaw's play a secondary thing. If our Patent is in danger, it is because the decisions of the English Censor are being brought into Ireland, and because the Lord Lieutenant is about to revive, on what we consider a frivolous pretext, a right not exercised for a hundred and fifty years to forbid, at the Lord Chamberlain's pleasure, any play produced in any Dublin theatre, all these theatres holding their Patents from him.

"We are not concerned with the question of the English Censorship now being fought out in London, but we are very certain that the conditions of the two countries are different, and that we must not, by accepting the English Censor's ruling, give away anything of the liberty of the Irish Theatre of the future. Neither can we accept without protest the revival of the Lord Lieutenant's claim at the bidding of the Censor or otherwise. The Lord Lieutenant is definitely a political personage, holding office from the party in power, and what would sooner or later grow into a political Censorship cannot be lightly accepted."

Having sent this out for publication, we went on with our rehearsals.

In rehearsal I came to think that there was a passage that would really seem irreverent and give offence to the genuinely religious minds we respect. It was where Blanco said: "Yah! What about the croup? I guess He made the croup when He was thinking of one thing; and then He made the child when He was thinking of something else; and the croup got past Him and killed the child. Some of us will have to find out how to kill the croup, I guess. I think I 'll turn doctor just on the chance of getting back on Him by doing something He could n't do."

I wrote to Mr. Shaw about this, and he answered in this very interesting letter:

"Parknasilla, 19 August, 1909.

"I have just arrived and found all your letters waiting for me. I am naturally much entertained by your encounters and Yeats' with the Castle. I leave that building cheerfully in your hands.

"But observe the final irony of the situation. The English Censorship being too stupid to see the real blasphemy, makes a fool of itself. But you, being clever enough to put your finger on it at once, immediately proceed to delete what Redford's blunders spared.

"To me, of course, the whole purpose of the play lies in the problem, 'What about the croup?" When Lady——, in her most superior manner, told me, 'He is the God of Love,' I said, 'He is also the God of Cancer and Epilepsy.' That does not present any difficulty to me. All this problem of the origin of evil, the mystery of pain, and so forth, does not puzzle me. My doctrine is that God proceeds by the method of 'Trial and error,' just like a workman perfecting an aëroplane; he has to make hands for himself and brains for himself in order that his will may be done. He has tried lots of machines—the diphtheria bacillus the tiger, the cockroach; and he cannot extirpate them, except by making something that can shoot them, or walk on them, or, cleverer still, devise vaccines and anti-toxins to prey on them. To me the sole hope of human salvation lies in teaching Man to regard himself as an experiment in the realisation of God, to regard his hands as God's hands, his brain as God's brain, his purpose as

God's purpose. He must regard God as a helpless longing, which *longed* him into existence by its desperate need for an executive organ. You will find it all in *Man and Super Man*, as you will find it all behind *Blanco Posnet*. Take it out of my play, and the play becomes nothing but the old cry of despair—Shakespeare's, 'As flies to wanton boys, so we are to the Gods; they kill us for their sport'—the most frightful blasphemy ever uttered." Mr. Shaw enclosed with this the passage rewritten, as it now appears in the published play.

We put on *Blanco* on the date announced, the 25th of August. We were anxious to the last, for counsel were of the opinion that if we were stopped, it would be on the Clause in the Patent against "Any representation which should be deemed or construed immoral," and that if Archbishop Walsh or Archbishop Peacocke or especially the Head of the Lord Lieutenant's own Church, the Moderator of the Presbyterian Assembly, should say anything which might be "deemed and construed" to condemn the play, the threats made would be carried out. There were fears of a riot also, for newspapers and their posters had kept up the excitement, and there was an immense audience. It is a pity we had not thought in time of putting up our prices. Guineas were offered even for standing room in the wings.

The play began, and till near the end it was received in perfect silence. Perhaps the audience were waiting for the wicked bits to begin. Then, at the end, there was a tremendous burst of cheering, and we knew we had won. Some stranger outside asked what was going on in the Theatre. "They are defying the Lord Lieutenant" was the answer; and when the crowd heard the cheering, they took it up and it went far out through the streets.

There were no protests made on any side. And the play, though still forbidden in England, is still played by us, and always with success. And even if the protests hoped for had been made and we had suffered, does not Nietzsche say "A good battle justifies every cause"?

CHAPTER VII

"THE PLAYBOY" IN AMERICA

On September 7, 1911, I received a letter from Mr. Yeats: "I am trying possible substitutes for Miss O'Neill and some will not do. As a last resource I have told Miss Magee to understudy the part of 'Pegeen Mike.' She was entirely natural and delightful in that small part in *The Mineral Workers* the day before yesterday. I said to some one that she had the sweet of the apple, and would be a Pegeen Mike if she could get the sour of the apple too. Now the serious difficulty of the moment is that there is nobody in the theatre capable of teaching a folk part to an inexperienced person. If there was, I would at once put Miss Magee into Pegeen Mike; by the time she had played it through the States she could come back Miss O'Neill's successor. Now, I am going to ask you if you feel well enough for a desperate measure. Can you, if it seem necessary to-morrow, take my place in the steamboat on Tuesday evening? Allowing eight days for the passage—for the boat is slow—you would arrive in Boston on the 20th. *The Playboy* cannot come till about the 28th; you would be able to train Miss Magee for the part, or, of course, another if you prefer her. . . . I can wire to-morrow and get the necessary papers made out (you have to swear you are not an Anarchist). If they want me I can follow next boat and possibly arrive before you. I will go steerage if necessary; that will be quite an amusing adventure, and I shall escape all interviewers. One thing I am entirely sure of, that there is no one but you with enough knowledge of folk to work a miracle."

I could not set out on the same day as the Company. I was needed at home. But I promised to follow in the *Cymric*, sailing from Queenstown a week later.

I think from the very first day Mr. Yeats and I had talked at Duras of an Irish Theatre, and certainly ever since there had been a company of Irish players, we had hoped and perhaps determined to go to *An t-Oilean ur* "the New Island," the greater Ireland beyond the Atlantic. But though, as some Connacht girls said to me at Buffalo, "Since ever we were the height of the table, America it was always our dream," and though we had planned that if for any cause our Theatre should seem to be nearing its end we would take our reserve fund and spend it mainly on that voyage and that venture, we did not ourselves make the opportunity at the last. After we had played in the summer of 1911 at the Court Theatre, as ever for a longer period and to a larger audience, we were made an offer by the theatrical managers, Liebler & Co., to play for three or four months in the United States, and the offer had been accepted. They had mentioned certain plays as essential, among them *The Playboy of the Western World.* Miss O'Neill, who had played its heroine, had married and left us; that is how the difficulty had arisen.

On September 19th I said good-bye to home, where I had meant to spend a quiet winter, writing and planting trees, and to the little granddaughter for whose first appearance in the world I had waited. There had not been many days for preparation, but it was just as well I did not require large trunks, for on the eve of my journey a railway strike was declared in Ireland and there were no trains to take any one to Queenstown. Motors are still few in the country. We wired to Limerick but all were engaged already; to Galway which did not answer at all; and to Loughrea, where the only one had already been engaged by my neighbour, Lord Gough, who had friends with him who also wanted means to travel. I could but send over a message to his home, Lough Cutra Castle, in the dark of night; and a kindly answer came that he would yield his claim to mine. So at midday on September 19th, I set out with such luggage as I could take, to cross the five counties that lay between me and Queenstown harbour. One of the tires broke at intervals, once on the top of a wild mountain in, I think, the County Limerick, and people came out from a lonely cottage to say how far we were from any town or help; and these delays kept us from reaching Cork till after dark. Then we went on towards Queenstown in a fine rain which had begun, and after a while when we stopped to ask the way we were told we had gone eight miles beyond it. But I was in time after all, went out in the tender and joined the *Cymric* next morning, and so made my first voyage across the ocean. The weather was rather cold and rough and I was glad of a rest, and stayed a good deal in my cabin. I knew no one on board and I had leisure to write a little play, *Mac Donough's Wife*, which had been forming itself in my mind for a while past.

I had always had a passion for the sea, as I saw it from our coasts and in our bays and invers, and when going through the Mediterranean and the Indian Ocean. But the great Atlantic seemed dark and dead and monotonous, and it was a relief when on the last day or two one could see whales spouting, and a sparrow came and perched on the ship; and then fishing boats, looking strange in shape and rigging, came in sight, and I felt like Christopher Columbus.

Mr. Yeats, who had gone on with the Company, came to meet me on board ship as we arrived at Boston on September 29th, St. Michael's Day, and told me of the success of the first performances there; and that evening I went to the Plymouth Theatre and found a large audience, and a very enthusiastic one, listening to the plays. I could not but feel moved when I saw this, and remembered our small beginnings and the years of effort and of discouragement.

The interviewers saved me the trouble of writing letters these first days. I sent papers home instead. It was my first experience of this way of giving news, and I was amused by it. One always, I suppose, likes talking about oneself and what one is interested in, and that is what they asked me to do. I found them everywhere courteous, mannerly, perhaps a litt e over-insistent. I think I only offended one, a lady in a provincial town. She wanted to talk about *The Playboy*, and for reasons of policy I did n't. She avenged herself by saying I had no sense of humour and that my dress (Paris!) "had no relation to the prevailing modes."

I had plenty to do at first. I had not much time to go about, for I rehearsed all the mornings and could not leave the theatre in the evenings, but when I got free of constant rehearsal I was taken by friends to see, as I longed to see, something of the country. I wanted especially to know what the coast here was like—whether it was very different from our own of Galway and of Clare; and I had a wonderful Sunday at a fine country house on the North Shore, and saw the islands and the reddish rocks, not like our grey ones opposite; and the lovely tints of the autumn leaves, a red and yellow undergrowth among the dark green trees. My hostess's grandchildren were playing about. One said, "I am going to be a bear," and grunted. It made me so glad to think the little grandson at home has a playfellow in the making—in the cradle!

Boston is a very friendly place. There are so many Irish there that I had been told at home there is a part of it called Galway, and I met many old friends. Some I had known as children, sons of tenants and daughters, now comfortably settled in their own houses. I had known of the nearness of America before I came, for I remember asking an old woman at Kiltartan why her daughter who had been home on a visit had left her again, and she had said, "Ah, her teeth were troubling her and her dentist lives at Boston." England, on the other hand, seems a long way off, and there are many tears shed if a child goes even to a good post over the Channel. Two dear old ladies came to see me, daughters of an old steward of my father's. One of them said she used to "braid my hair" as a child that I might be in time for family prayers, and had wept when she saw the snapshots in the papers after I landed, and found I was so changed. She said, weeping, "I hope the people of America know you are a real lady; if not, I could testify to it!" And I was able to write to my son of the well-being of tenants' children: "T. C. and his wife came to the theatre and brought me a beautiful bouquet of pink carnations. I had a visit from M. R., such a handsome, smart girl, and from N. H., sending up her visiting card, very pleased with herself. Many of the ladies I meet tell me the cook or laundress or manservant are so excited at their meeting me and know all about me." And the son of a Welsh carpenter who had lived at Roxborough in my childhood met me at the theatre door after *Spreading the News* and said, "I never thought, when you used to teach us in Sunday School, you would ever write such merry comedies." This reminded me of the tailor from Gort who wrote home after a visit to the Abbey, "No one who knows Lady Gregory would ever think she had so much fun in her."

On October 8th I wrote home: "I send a paper with opinions for and against the plays. I am afraid there may be demonstrations against *Harvest* and *The Playboy*. The Liebler people don't mind, think it will be an advertisement. I was cheered by a visit from some members of the Gaelic League, saying they were on our side and asking me to an entertainment next Sunday, and from D. K., who is very religious and wants to go into a convent. She says the attacks on the plays are by very few and don't mean anything. Most of the society people are in the country, but they motor in sixty or eighty miles for the plays. Last night we had a little party on the stage: some Gaelic Leaguers, who brought me a bouquet; some people from the Aran colony—including Synge's friend, McDonough, whom I had also known in Aran; and from Kiltartan Mary R. and a cousin and Mrs. Hession's daughters, with the husband of one. They were very smart, one in a white blouse, another in a blue one with pearl necklace. You must tell Mrs. Hession they are looking so well. The management gave us sandwiches on the stage, and punchbowls of claret cup, and we had Irish songs and I called for a cheer for Ireland in Boston. I enjoyed very much watching the Hession women at the play. They nearly got hysterics in *Workhouse Ward*, and when the old woman comes on, they did not laugh but bent forward and took it quite seriously. It shows the plays would have a great success in the country. The County Galway Woman's League have asked me to be their president. . . . Members of the Gaelic League are working a banner for me. They showed me the painted design at a party given in our honour. Yeats leaves for New York to-day, but comes back for first night of *The Playboy* next Monday and sails Tuesday. They are rather afraid of trouble, but I think the less controversy the better now. It should be left between the management and the audience.

"The manager says we may stay longer in Boston, we are doing so well. I should like to stay on. It is a homey sort of place. I am sent quantities of flowers, my room is full of roses and carnations."

Now as to the trouble over *The Playboy*. We were told, when we arrived, that opposition was being organised from Dublin, and I was told there had already been some attacks in a Jesuit paper, *America*. But the first I saw was a letter in the

Boston Post of October 4th, the writer of which did not wait for *The Playboy* to appear but attacked plays already given, *Birthright* and *Hyacinth Halvey*. The letter was headed in large type, "Dr. J. T. Gallagher denounces the Irish Plays, says they are Vulgar, Unnatural, Anti-National, and Anti-Christian." The writer declared himself astonished at "the parrot-like praise of the dramatic critics." He himself had seen these two plays and "my soul cried out for a thousand tongues to voice my unutterable horror and disgust. . . . I never saw anything so vulgar, vile, beastly, and unnatural, so calculated to calumniate, degrade, and defame a people and all they hold sacred and dear."

Birthright, written by a young National schoolmaster in County Cork, had not been attacked in Ireland; both it and my own *Hyacinth* have been played not only at the Abbey but in the country towns and villages with the approval of the priests and of the Gaelic League. *Birthright* is founded on some of the most ancient of stories, Cain and Abel, Joseph and the pit, jealousy of the favoured younger by the elder, a sudden anger, and "the voice of thy brother's blood crieth to me from the ground." In a photograph of the last scene a Boston photographer had, to fill his picture, brought on the father and mother looking at the struggle between the brothers, instead of coming in, as in the play, to find but a lifeless body before them. This heartlessness was often brought up against us by some who had seen the picture but not the play, and sometimes by those who had seen both.

The Playboy was announced for October 16th, and on the 14th the *Gaelic American* printed a resolution of the United Irish Societies of New York, in which they pledged themselves to "drive the vile thing from the stage."

There was, however, very little opposition in the Plymouth Theatre. There was a little booing and hissing, but there were a great many Harvard boys among the audience and whenever there was a sign of coming disapproval they cheered enough to drown it. Then they took to cheering if any sentence or scene was coming that had been objected to in the newspaper attacks, so, I am afraid, giving the impression that they had a particular liking for strong expressions. We had, as I have already told, cut out many of these long ago in

Dublin, and had never put them back when we played in England or elsewhere; and so the enemy's paper confessed almost sadly, "it was a revised and amended edition that they saw . . . the most offensive parts were eliminated. It was this that prevented a riot. . . . But most of those present and all the newspaper men had read the excised portions in the *Gaelic American* and were able to fill the gaps."

Because of the attacks in some papers, the Mayor of Boston sent his secretary, Mr. William A. Leahy, to report upon *The Playboy*, and the Police Commissioners also sent their censor. Both reports agreed that the performance was not such as to "justify the elimination of any portion of the play." Mr. Leahy had already written of the other plays: "I have seen the plays and admire them immensely. They are most artistic, wonderfully acted, and to my mind absolutely inoffensive to the patriotic Irishman. I regret the sensitiveness that makes certain men censure them. Knowing what Mr. Yeats and Lady Gregory want to do, I cannot but hope that they succeed and that they are loyally supported in America. My commendation cannot be expressed too forcibly." And after he had seen *The Playboy*, he wrote: "If obscenity is to be found on the stage in Boston, it must be sought elsewhere and not at the Plymouth Theatre." After speaking with some sympathy of the objections made to the plays, he says: "The mistake, however, lies in taking the pictures literally. Some of these playwrights, of course, are realists or copyists of life and like others of their kind they happen to prefer strong brine to rosewater and see truth chiefly in the ugliness of things. But as it happens the two remarkable men among the Irish playwrights are not realists at all. Yeats and Synge are symbolists, and their plays are as fantastic and fabulous as the Tales of the Round Table."

There was no further trouble at Boston. There was nothing but a welcome for all the plays, many of them already so well known, especially through Professor Baker's dramatic classes at Harvard, that we were now and again reproved by some one in the audience if a line or passage were left out, by design or forgetfulness. I wrote home on October 22nd: "Gaston Mayer came yesterday, representing Liebler. They are delighted with our success, and want us, urged us, to stay till May. We refused this, but will certainly stay January, possibly a little longer. It is rather a question for the Company. They want me to stay all the time. I said I would stay for the present. If I get tired, Yeats will come back. . . . We had the sad news last night that we are only to have one more week here, and are to do some three night places, opening at Providence on the 30th. Mrs. Gardner came to the theatre this morning, furious at our going so soon."

We said farewell to Boston October 30th. Yet it was not quite farewell, for on our last day in America—March 5th—we stopped there on the way from Chicago to New York and gave a "flying matinée"; and I brought home the impression of that kind, crowded audience, and the knowledge that having come among strangers, we left real friends.

On October 13th I had written from Boston: "I am sorry to say Flynn (Liebler's special agent), who has been to Providence, announces strong opposition to *The Playboy.* A delegation came to demand its withdrawal, but he refused. I had also a letter saying the Clan-na-Gael was very strong there, and advising that we have police at hand. Of course, had we known this, we should not have put on *The Playboy*, but we must fight it out now. The danger is in not knowing whether we shall get any strong support there. A Harvard lad has interviewed me for a magazine. He promised to try and make up a party to go to Providence Tuesday night, and also to stir up Brown University."

Though we all grieved at leaving friendly Boston, we found friends also at Providence, with its pleasant name and hilly streets and stately old dwelling houses. But a protest had been made before we arrived, and a committee had waited on the Police Commissioners and presented a petition asking them to forbid the performance of *The Playboy*.

"I had to appear before the Police Commissioners this morning. The accusations were absurd and easy to answer; most of them founded upon passages which have never been said upon the stage. I wish I had been allowed to take a copy. There was one clause which accused us of 'giving the world to understand a barbarous marriage custom was in ordinary use in Ireland.' This alluded to the 'drift of chosen females from the Eastern World,' one of those flights of Christy Mahon's fancy which have given so much offence. I showed them the prompt copy with the acting version we have always used. Unluckily the enemy did n't turn up. Of course the play is to be let go on, and there are to be plenty of policemen present in case of disturbance. The police people said they had had the same trouble about a negro play said to misrepresent people of colour.

"The Police Commissioners themselves attended and have published a report, saying they not only found nothing to object to in the play but enjoyed every minute of it. Nevertheless, the protesting committee published its statement: 'How well our objections were founded may be judged from the fact that the Company acting this play has agreed to eliminate from it each and every scene, situation, and word to which we objected, and it is on the basis of this elimination that the play has been permitted to go on.' And I gave my answer: 'I think it may be as well to state that we gave the play to-night exactly as it has been given in London, Oxford, Cambridge, Manchester, and many cities in Ireland and the other night in

Boston. The players have never at any time anywhere spoken all the lines in the published book.'" And after its production I wrote home: "Nov. 1st. *The Playboy* went very well last night, not an attempt to hiss."

From another town—Lowell—I wrote: "A newspaper man from Tyrone lamented last night the *Playboy* fight. He said all nationalities here are very sensitive. The Swedes had a play taken off that represented some Swedish women drinking. The French Canadians, he says, are as touchy as the Irish. He said that in consequence of this sensitiveness, in the police reports the nationality of those brought up before the court is not given. I looked in the Lowell newspaper next day, and I saw that this was true. One José Viatchka was brought up charged with the theft of two yards of cloth. She was found guilty and her nationality was not given. Allan Carter made his second appearance for drunkenness. Being an American citizen, even his dwelling place, Canaan, N. H., was not kept secret. Thomas Kilkelly and Daniel O'Leary were fined for drunkenness. I felt very glad that their nationality was not given!"

Yale like Harvard demanded *The Playboy*, and we put it on for one night at New Haven. Synge's plays and others on our list are being used in the course of English literature there, and professors and students wanted to see them. We were there for Monday and Tuesday, the 6th and 7th of November. On the first night we put on other plays. Next day there was a matinée and we gave Mr. Bernard Shaw's *Blanco Posnet* and my own *Image*. I left before the matinée was over for Northampton, as I was to lecture that night at Smith College. Next day I was astonished to see a paragraph in a New Haven paper, saying that the Mayor, having been asked to forbid the performance of *The Playboy*, had sent his censor, the Chief of Police, Mr. Cowles, to attend a rehearsal of it; that several passages had been objected to by him and that the manager had in consequence suppressed them, and it had been given at the evening performance without the offending passages. I was astounded. I knew the report could not be correct, must be wholly incorrect, and yet one knows there is never smoke without even a sod of turf. The players, who arrived at Northampton that morning, were equally puzzled. There had been no rehearsal, and the play had been given as ever before. I wired to a friend, the head of the University Press at Yale, to investigate the matter. The explanation came: "Chief Cowles," as the papers called him, had attended, not a rehearsal but the matinée. He was said to have objected to certain passages, though he had not sent word of this to any of our people. The passages he objected to were not spoken at the evening performance of *The Playboy*, because the play in which they are spoken was *Blanco Posnet*. Yale laughed over this till we could almost hear the echoes, indeed the echoes appeared in the next day's papers. *The Gaelic American*, however, announced that in New Haven one of our plays "was allowed to be presented only after careful excision of obscene passages."

Washington was the next place where *The Playboy* was to appear. I wrote home from there on November 12th: "Liebler's Manager wired for me to come on here and skip Albany. To-day two or three priests preached against us, and a pamphlet has been given away at the chapel doors denouncing us. I think it would be a good thing to put it up in the Hall of the Abbey framed for

Dublin people to see. The worst news is that the players have arrived without Sinclair. He had a fall down six steps when coming down to the stage at Albany and hurt his back. The doctor said it was only the muscles that were hurt and that he would be all right to-day, but he has wired to-day that he cannot move. A bad performance would worry me more than the pamphlet.

"These are some of its paragraphs:

"'The attention of fair-minded Washingtonians is called to a most malignant travesty of Irish life and religion about to be presented upon the stage of a local theatre by the "Irish Players." This travelling Company is advertised as "coming from the Abbey Theatre, Dublin." True, but they came from Dublin, followed by the hisses and indignation of an outraged populace!

"'A storm of bitter protest has been raised in every city in which they have presented their false and revolting pictures of Irish life. Dublin people never accepted the plays. They virtually kicked them from the stage. England gave them no reception.'

"Then they quote 'a Boston critic' (this is Dr.

Gallagher, who wrote that letter to the Boston papers):

"'"Nothing but hell-inspired ingenuity and a satanic hatred of the Irish people and their religion could suggest, construct, and influence the production of such plays. On God's earth the beastly creatures of the plays never existed."

"'Such are the productions which, hissed from Dublin, hawked around England by the "Irish Players" for the delectation of those who wished to see Irishmen shown unfit for self-government, are now offered to the people of Washington. Will Washington tolerate the lie?

"'THE ALOYSIUS TRUTH SOCIETY.'

"This is the first time any section of the Catholic Church has come into the fight. It is a good thing they denounce all the plays, not only *The Playboy*. On the other hand, the Gaelic Association, of which Monsignor Shahan, President of the Catholic University, is head, has asked me to address its meeting next Thursday, and, of course, I shall do so.

"This invitation was incorrectly reported in the papers, and Monsignor Shahan, who is just leaving for Rome, has denied having 'invited the

Irish Players to speak.' The invitations sent out, printed cards with his printed signature, had asked people to come and hear me speak, and I did so and had a good audience; and a resolution was proposed, praising all I had done for literature and the theatre, and making me the first Honorary Member of the Association, and this was agreed to by the whole meeting with applause."

For among the surprises of the autumn I had suddenly found that I could speak. I was quite miserable when, on arriving in Boston, I found it had been arranged for me to "say a few words" at various clubs or gatherings. I thought a regular lecture would be better. If it failed, I would not be asked again or I would have an excuse for silence. It would be easier, too, in a way than the "few words," for I should know how long the lecture ought to be and what people wanted to hear about, and I would have the assurance that they knew what they were coming for instead of having a stranger let loose on them just as they were finishing their lunch. It was at one of these lunches that that wonderful woman who has in Boston, as the Medici in Florence, spent wealth and vitality and knowledge in making such a collection of noble pictures as proves once more that it is the individual, the despot, who is necessary for such a task—bringing the clear conception, the decision of one mind in place of the confusion of many—liked what I said and offered me for my first trial the spacious music room of Fenway Court.

I spoke on playwriting, for I had begun that art so late in life that its rules, those I had worked out for myself or learned from others, were still fresh in my mind; and I wrote home with more cheerfulness than I had felt during the days of preparation, that I thought and was assured my address had gone well; "what I was most proud of was keeping it exactly to the hour. I was glad to find I could fill up so much time. I had notes on the table and just glanced at them now and again but did n't hesitate for a word or miss my points. It is a great relief to me and the discovery of a new faculty. I shan't feel nervous again; that is a great thing."

I had boasted of this a little too soon, for the next letter says: "I had a nice drive yesterday, twenty-five miles to B. A lady called for me in her motor, and we passed through several pretty little New England villages and through woods. Then a wait of an hour before lecture, keeping up small talk and feeling nervous all the time, then the lecture. I forgot to bring my watch and gave them twenty minutes over the hour! It was a difficult place to speak in, a private house,—a room to the right, a room to the left, and a room behind. However they seemed to hear all right. . . . I had a nice run home alone in the dark."

I gave my ideas on "playwriting" again at Philadelphia, and was told just before I began that there were several dramatists in the room, including the author of *Madame Butterfly*. So I had to apologise on the ground of an inferior cook being flattered at being asked to give recipes, whereas a real *chef* keeps the secrets to himself. And sometimes at the end of all my instruction on the rules I gave the hearers as a benediction,

> "And may you better reck the rede
> Than ever did the adviser!"

Mr. Yeats, when lecturing in America, had written to me from Bryn Mawr: "I have just given my second lecture. . . . They are getting all our books here now. Do you know I have not met a single woman here who puts 'tin-tacks in the soup,' and I find that the woman who does, is recognised as an English type. One teacher explained to me the difference in this way: 'We prepare the girls to live their lives, but in England they are making them all teachers.'"

And I also was delighted with the girls' colleges and wrote home:

"At Vassar the girls were playing a football game in sympathy with the Harvard and Yale match going on. They were all dressed as boys, had made up trousers, or knickers, and some were playing on combs to represent a band, and singing the Yale song, though the sham Harvard had beaten the sham Yale by 25 to 5. They are nice, merry girls, I think as nice as at Smith's, where I promised to suggest my granddaughter should be educated. I had an audience of about six hundred, a very good and pleasant one, nearly all girls and a few men. The President was sitting close to the door, and I asked him to call out to me to speak up if he did n't hear, as I was young as a lecturer and always afraid my voice might not reach. He said he would not like to do that, but would hold up a handkerchief if I was to speak louder. About the middle of the lecture I saw him very slowly raise a handkerchief to the level of his face, but I could not catch his eye, so I stopped and asked if that was the signal. He was quite confused and said, No, he wanted to blow his nose, and the girls shrieked with delight. He told me afterwards he had held out as long as he could. The girls had acted some of my plays. *The Jackdaw* is a great favourite there as well as at Smith's, where they have conjugated a verb 'to Jackdaw.' One of the 'Faculty' said she doubted if our players could do *Gaol Gate* as well as Mr. Kennedy, the author of *The Servant in the House*, reads it. . . ."

These lectures gave me opportunity of seeing many places where our plays did not go, and I have delighted memories of rushing waters in Detroit, and of little girls dancing in cruciform Columbus, and of the roar of Niagara Falls, and the stillness of the power house that sends that great energy to create light and motion a hundred or two hundred miles away, and of many another wide-spreading, kindly city where strangers welcomed me, and I seemed to say good-bye to friends. Dozing in midnight trains, I would remember, as in a dream, "the flight of a bird through a lighted hall," the old parable of human life.

To return to the meeting at Washington:

"I had to get away early because Mrs. Taft had asked me to the White House to hear the Mormon choir. I arrived there rather late but the music was going on. It was a very pretty sight, the long white room with fine old glass chandeliers, and two hundred Mormons—the men in black, the women in white—and about fifty guests. I heard one chorus, and they sang 'The Star-Spangled Banner,' and everyone stood up. Then we moved about and chatted, and I was presented to the President—pleasant enough, but one doesn't feel him on the stage like Roosevelt.

"To-day I had a very scattered rehearsal of *Spreading the News*. The players kept slipping out by a back door, and I found the negroes were dancing and singing out there, it being their dinner hour. It was, of course, irresistible."

One day when we went to rehearsal, the sun was shining and I offered the players a holiday and picnic to Mount Vernon, and we crossed the river and spent the day there very pleasantly.

Donovan said, "No wonder a man should fight for such a home as this." I told them the holiday was not a precedent, for we might go to a great many countries before finding so great a man to honour. Washington had been a friend of my grandfather's, who had been in America with his regiment. There was a case of stuffed birds at Roxborough which was said to have been a present from Washington, and there was a field there called Mount Vernon. My grandfather had built a little sea lodge on the Burren coast and had called that also Mount Vernon, so I was specially interested in seeing the house. It is beautifully kept and filled with memorials of its owner and with furniture that belonged to him. The Americans keep their sacred places well. A school at which I lectured wanted to give me a fee; but I did not wish to take one, and I said when they pressed it, that I had seen in a shop window an old jug with portraits of Washington and of Lafayette on it, and had wished for it, but it was nine dollars and I was refraining from luxuries, and that I would accept that if they liked. So it was sent to me, and I brought it safely home to add to my collection of historic delft. It has the date 1824. It was made to commemorate Lafayette's visit at that time, and the words on it are, "A Republic is not always ungrateful." It now stands near another jug of about the same date, on which there is the portrait of that other patriot beloved by his people, O'Connell.

On November 18th I arrived at New York. All my work was easier from that time through the help of my friend of some ten years, Mr. John Quinn. I had a pleasant little set of rooms at the Algonquin Hotel. I said to Mr. Flynn, Liebler's manager, when I arrived there, "Is it near the theatre? Shall I be able to walk there?" "Walk there," he said, "why you could throw a cricket ball to it." I did walk there and back many times a day during my stay, and grew fond of the little corner of the city I got to know so well; but I sometimes envied the cricket ball that would have escaped the dangerous excitement of the five crossings, one of them across 6th Avenue, with motors dashing in all directions, and railway trains thundering overhead. The theatre was charming, I wish we could carry it about on all our tours, and I was given a little room off the stage, which had been

Maxine Elliott's own room, and where players and guests often had tea with me.

"Hotel Algonquin, New York, Monday, 20th November. We opened very well last night. A crowded house and very enthusiastic, *Rising of the Moon*, *Birthright*, and *Spreading the News* were given. All got five or more curtains. One man made rather a disturbance at the fight in *Birthright*, saying it was 'not Irish,' but his voice was drowned and he left. I was told that —— one of the enemy who was there, said, 'Such things do not happen in Ireland; they may happen in Lady Gregory's own family.' *The Playboy* is to be put on next week. J. Q. seems a bit anxious about *The Playboy;* says they may 'throw things,' and that seems what the *Gaelic American* is inviting them to do when it says *The Playboy* 'must be squelched' and a lesson taught to Mr. Yeats and his fellow-agents of England, and that I have no right to appeal for respect for my sex.

"Last night as I went into the theatre I heard my name spoken, and a girl told me she was the daughter of old Matt Cahel, the blacksmith who had lived at Roxborough, and she had come to see the plays and said her father would have been so proud, if he had lived, to know I was here. I am glad of this, for I hear the plays were preached against by some priests last Sunday. Father Flanagan thinks the attacks all come from Dublin. The players are convinced they are from some of our non-paying guests. . . . I think we must revise that list. *The Playboy* is to be put on next Monday. I am glad they are not putting off the fight any longer. It tries the players' nerves. It will be on for four nights and a matinée. By going behind myself and gathering a party and cheering with what voice I had left, I at last got the shouts for Hughie in *Birthright* to be less of a mournful wail."

"Friday, November 24th. I have been to-day to lunch with Mrs. ——, a Catholic lady I had met in London, who gave a lunch to me to show she was on our side. There was a Father X. there, who is not in this diocese and is very much shocked at the action of the priests. One told his congregation on Sunday from the altar, it would be a mortal sin to come to the plays, and another, Father X. says, to his certain knowledge advised his people from the altar if they did come, to bring eggs to throw. Mr. Hackett was sitting behind a woman who said in *Birthright* 'it 's a pity it ain't Lady Gregory they are choking.' Mr. Quinn heard I held a salon at the theatre and it is wonderful how many people turn up or come to express sympathy. I got a good rehearsal to-day of *Mixed Marriage*, which I think might take very well here."

"26th. Plenty of booking for *Playboy* whether by friends or enemies. I went to lecture at Vassar yesterday. I had no idea the Hudson was so beautiful. The train was close to the brink all the way, and opposite are wooded cliffs and heights, and at night, coming back, the lighted towns on the other side gave a magic atmosphere. I find new scenery an extraordinary excitement and delight. I am going off just now to Oyster Bay for the night to visit the Roosevelts. I have been to church this morning and feel fresher."

"Algonquin, Monday, 27th. When John Quinn came yesterday afternoon, he brought Gregg with him. Both had heard from different sources that *The Playboy* is to be attacked to-night. The last *Gaelic American* says, 'The New York Irish will send the Anti-Irish Players back to Dublin like whipped curs with their tails between their legs.' Quinn heard it from a man he knows well, who had called him up to say there is a party of rowdies coming to the theatre to-night to make their demonstration. They thought it possible this might be stopped by letting the enemy know we are prepared, but I thought it better to let them show themselves. They have been threatening us so long; we shall see who they are.

"This morning I saw Flynn and Gaston Mayer and told them the matter was out of my hands now, that we don't want interviews or argument, and that it is a question between Liebler and the mob. Flynn went off to the police, and I have not heard anything since. I have not told the players."

"Tuesday, November 28th. The papers give a fairly accurate account of what happened last night.[1] There was a large audience, *The Gaol Gate* was put on first, which, of course, has never offended anyone in Ireland, but there was a good deal of coughing going on and there was unrest in the gallery. But one man was heard saying to another, 'This is all right. You need n't

[1] See extract in appendix.

interrupt this. Irishmen do die for their neighbours.' Another said, 'This is a part of *The Playboy* that is going on now, but they are giving it under another name.' Very soon after the curtain went up on *The Playboy* the interruptions began. The managers had been taking much too confident a view, saying, 'These things don't happen in New York.' When this did happen, there were plenty of police, but they would n't arrest anyone becausc no one gave the order, and the disturbance was let go on nearly all through the first act. I went round, when the disturbance began, and knelt in the opening of the hearth, calling to every actor who came within earshot that they must not stop for a moment but must spare their voices, as they could not be heard, and we should do the whole act over again. At the end Tyler came round and I was delighted when he shouted that it should be played again. O'Donovan announced this and there were great cheers from the audience. And the whole play was given then in perfect peace and quiet. The editor of the *Gaelic American* and his bodyguard were in the stalls, two rows of them. They were pointed out to me when I came in. The disturbers were very well arranged; little groups here and there. In the box office this morning they have a collection of spoils left by the enemy (chiefly stink-pots and rosaries). A good many potatoes were thrown on the stage and an old watch, and a tin box with a cigar in it and a cigarette box. Our victory was complete in the end.

"Ten men were arrested. Two of them were bar-tenders; one a liquor dealer; two clerks; one a harness-maker; one an instructor; one a mason; one a compositor, and one an electrician.

"Some of the police who protected us were Irish. One of them said to our manager, Mr. Robinson: 'There 's a Kerryman says he has you pictured and says he 'll have your life.' Mr. Robinson had had some words with this Kerryman and had said: 'We 'll give you a supper when you come to Dublin,' and the Kerryman had answered, 'We 'll give you a wake.'

"The disturbers were fined sums from three to ten dollars each."

"28th. I was talking to Roosevelt about the opposition on Sunday and he said he could not get in to the plays: Mrs. Roosevelt not being well, he did not like to leave home. But when I said it would be a help to us, he said, 'Then I will certainly come,' and settled that to-night he will dine with me and come on."

"Wednesday, 29th. I was in such a rush last night I sent off my letters very untidily. I had n't time even to change my dress for dinner. It went off very well. John Quinn, Col. Emmet, grand-nephew of the Patriot, Mr. Flynn. I had asked Peter Dunne (Mr. Dooley) but he was engaged to dinner at eight at the Guinnesses. He came, however, at seven and sat through ours. He was very amusing, and he and Roosevelt chaffed each other. . . . When we got to the theatre and into the box, people saw Roosevelt and began to clap and at last he had to get up, and he took my hand and dragged me on my feet too, and there was renewed clapping. . . . Towards the end of *Gaol Gate* there was a great outbreak of coughing and sneezing, and then there was a scuffle in the gallery and a man throwing pepper was put out. There was a scuffle now and then during *The Playboy* but nothing violent and always great clapping when the offender was thrown out. We played with the lights up. After the first act I took my party on to the stage and introduced the players, and Roosevelt spoke separately to them and then made a little speech, saying how much he admired them and that he felt they were doing a great deal to increase the dignity of Ireland (he has adopted my phrase) and that he 'envied them and Lady Gregory for America.' They were quite delighted and Kerrigan had tears in his eyes. Roosevelt's daughter, who was with another party, then appeared and he introduced her to them, remembering all the names, 'This is Mr. Morgan, this is Miss Magee. . . .' I brought him a cup of tea and it was hard to tear him away when the curtain went up.

"I stayed in my room writing letters through the second act, and when I came back, a swarm of reporters was surrounding Roosevelt and he was declaring from the box, 'I would as soon discuss the question as discuss a pipe dream with an out-patient of Bedlam.' This was about an accusation they had just shown him in some paper, saying he had had a secret understanding with some trusts. He was shaking his fist and saying, 'I am giving you that straight; mind you, take it down as I say it.' When the play was over, he stayed in the box a few minutes discussing it;

he said he would contribute a note on an article he wants John Quinn to write about us. When we left the box, we found the whole route to the door packed, just a narrow lane we could walk through, and everyone taking off hats and looking at him with real reverence and affection, so unlike those royal crowds in London. It was an extraordinary kindness that he did us."

The Mayor had received a protest against the play and on that second night he sent as his representative the Chief Magistrate, Mr. McAdoo, who had formerly been a member of Congress, had served as Assistant Secretary of the Navy and as Police Commissioner of New York, and is a leading citizen of the city.

The *New York Sun*, in the issue of November 30th, summarised his report:

"Chief Magistrate McAdoo, who was sent by Mayor Gaynor on Tuesday night to see *The Playboy of the Western World*, wrote to the Mayor yesterday that he had sat through the play and had seen nothing in it to warrant the fuss which some Irishmen were making. Magistrate McAdoo told the Mayor that it was not nearly as objectionable as scores of American plays he had seen in this city and that there was no reason why the Mayor should either order the withdrawal of the play or suspend the licence of Maxine Elliott's Theatre. The Mayor said that the letter had satisfied him that there was no need of any action by the city and that so far as he was concerned the matter was closed."

"Of the few arrested on the second night one was an Englishman, who objected to British soldiers being spoken of as 'khaki cut-throats,' and one was a Jew, who did not give his reasons. For the accusations were getting more and more mixed. A man was heard asking outside the Maxine Elliott Theatre during the riot, 'What is on to-night?' and the answer was, 'There 's a Jew-man inside has a French play and he 's letting on it 's Irish, and some of the lads are inside talking to them.'

"I have had a nice letter from Rothenstein. He is here painting some portraits. He says, 'I would have been to pay you my respects but unhappily I have for the second time been laid up. I hope I may still get the chance, and that the charming and brilliant people I saw with such delight in London are getting their due. I want to bring some friends to see them this week, and am looking forward to the pleasure of seeing them again.' This was written on the morning of the 28th, and he adds a postscript: 'Since writing I see at breakfast an account of a big fuss you had last night. I think it is a fine thing that a work of art should have so vital an effect on people that they feel towards it as they do towards life, and wish to exalt or to destroy it. In these days when there is so little understanding of the content and so much said about the technique of these things, I do feel refreshed that such a thing can happen. I hope the physical experience was not too trying. I admire the courage and determination which both sides showed. If a country can produce so great a man as Synge and a public so spirited that it will protest against what seems a wrong presentment of life to them, then we may still have hope that art will find a place by the fireside. I take my hat off to you all.'"

"December 1st. All well last night. Galleries filled, and apparently with Irish, all applauding, not one hiss.

"I was asked at a tea-party 'what was my moral purpose in writing *The Playboy!*'"

Mr. Yeats wrote from Dublin when he heard of the riot: "December 3d. What a courageous man Roosevelt is! I mean courageous to go so much beyond official routine. I think it is the best thing that has ever happened to us so far as opinion here is concerned. The papers here have been exceedingly venomous. I am having a baize-covered board with a glass frame to fit in it put up in the vestibule, and promised the audience yesterday, speaking from the stage, that I would put up the American notices as they reached us, good and bad alike. At present I have put up an old picture frame with the rather lengthy London notices of the row., I think it wise that our own people should know that they see there on the board some proof of the reception we are getting. . . . Shaw has just sent me a copy of an interview he is sending to the *New York Sun*. He says you are 'the greatest living Irishwoman,' and adds you will beat the Clan na Gael as you beat the Castle. He makes a most amusing and ferocious attack on the Clan na Gael, and says they are not Irish. . . . But I forgot, you will have read it before this reaches you. I hope he will not have left you all in the plight the little boy was in after

Don Quixote had beaten his master. He will, at any rate, have amused New York, which does not care for the Clan, and all fuel helps when one wants a fire. I am pleased that he has seen the issue—that we are the true Ireland fighting the false."

I wrote home on December 1st. "The Company have signed on till end of February, so I shall most likely stay till then. The only thing I am at all afraid of is want of sleep. I don't get much. Everyone says the climate here is exciting, but I may get used to it, and we have had exciting times.

"I have made my little room off the stage into a greenroom, and brought some books there and made regular arrangements for tea. There are no greenrooms in these theatres and the Company look rather miserable straying about. Mrs. G. is lending me her motor this afternoon and I am taking some of the players for a drive and to Quinn's for tea. He is such a help to me, so capable and kind. My December horoscope, I remember, said, 'Benefit through friends' and I think it comes about a month wrong and that things happen in the previous month, for in November I had help from him and Bernard Shaw and Roosevelt!

"A priest came in yesterday to express his sympathy, and attended the plays, and I took him round to see the players. So far 'the Church' has not pronounced against us, only individual priests. . . . The servant maids are told we are 'come to mock Ireland.' We are answering nothing now, just going on. Bernard Shaw's article is splendid, going to the root of the matter, as you say. I am just now going over to the theatre to see the start of the voice-production classes. . . . I determined there should be a beginning."

"Dec. 12th. The luncheon with the *Outlook* was great fun. There were present the editors, an Admiral, and some other military heroes, and after lunch some one called for silence 'that Lady Gregory might be questioned.' So they asked questions from here and there, and I gave answers. For instance, they asked if the riot had affected our audience, and I said, yes, I was afraid more people had come to see us pelted than playing. And that I had met a few nights before in Buffalo a General Green, who told me that when driving through crowds cheering for Roosevelt, he had said to

Roosevelt, 'Theodore, don't you feel elated by this?' And Mr. Roosevelt had said, 'Frank, I always keep in mind what the Duke of Wellington said on a similar occasion, "How many more would come to see me hanged"' (great applause). . . . Someone asked me why I had worked so hard at the Theatre, and I quoted Blake:

> I will not cease from mental strife
> Or let the sword fall from my hand
> Till we have built Jerusalem
> In—Ireland's—fair and lovely land.

"For, I said, it was a part of the building of Jerusalem. This went very well, and in my lecture at Brooklyn in the evening I tried it again, but it was received with roars of delighted laughter. It was explained to me afterwards that a part of Brooklyn is full of Jews, who are trying to turn it into a Jerusalem of their own!

"Oh, I am tired to-night!"

"Dec. 15th. Mrs. ——, the Catholic friend who is working for us, is sending to-day to the *Tablet* a very good notice of us written by a priest. She says educated priests and Catholics generally are so much ashamed of the riot that they give out it was got up by the management! She wanted me to have this contradicted, but of course it would be useless. I have just had the *Outlook* and will send it on to you. Roosevelt 'commanded' Quinn to write an article on us. He said he could n't, but I think it is charming."

"Sunday, 27th. I don't think the Church will really turn on us. It would bring it into a fight with all the theatres and that would make it unpopular. Here Catholics take care to say, 'It is not the Church that is against you, only certain priests.' Father Y. telephoned me this afternoon, saying he was praying for us every day and for the success of our work, and that he thinks *Workhouse Ward* as fine as Shakespeare! Another priest, Father Z., Chaplain in the Navy, has asked me to tea, and says he will come to see the plays, only not *The Playboy*."

"A nice matinée yesterday. My friend the wild Irishman who comes to the theatre, tells me the Irish are 'waiting for us' in Chicago, but I don't see what they can do.

"The *Gaelic American* is firing a very distant and random gun now though it has headed an article '*Playboy* as dead as a nail in a door.' I have just been reading Masefield's *Everlasting Mercy*. How fine it is, as fine as *Nan*, but leading to Heaven and the wholesomeness of earth instead of poison pies!

"Mrs. —— gave a tea for me yesterday, and people seemed enthusiastic and there is evidently a great deal of talk about us; but it is just like London, we are building downwards from the intellectuals. *Image* went so well last night I was glad I had put it on. Quinn was delighted with the scene and grouping. He thought each scene like an Augustus John drawing. . . . I believe the critics are bewildered because of so much new work. Priests keep dropping in and seem to enjoy the plays, and O'S. told me last night all the young men are either coming to see us or if they have no money, are reading our plays at the library and getting up debates concerning them.

"A lady at Philadelphia said to another, 'What did you really think of *Lady Gregory's* play, *The "Cowboy" of the Western World!*'

"Many happy New Years to you!"

"December 29th. I am too tired to write a letter. This is just to say all is going well, big houses on these last nights. *Kathleen* and *The*

Playboy both go extremely well. We have got the audience, and I believe, and everyone says, we could now run on for weeks, but the theatre is let to someone else. It is just as well leaving at the top of the wave. Next week six towns, then Philadelphia.

"January 2d. I had a talk with Tyler. He was nice, and they want us to confirm the contract for next year. Talking of the opposition he said, 'The Irish seem to be always afraid of things.' . . . Last week was a real triumph."

"Philadelphia, January 9, 1912. I am staying here with Mr. and Mrs. Jayne, in a beautiful house, with great kindness from my host and hostess. We opened very well last night. We had a very appreciative audience. Mr. and Mrs. —— afterwards gave a supper for me and presented me with an immense basket of roses.

"We dined on Sunday night with Dr. Furness, the old Shakesperean scholar. We went by rail and had to walk a little way to his house. It was four degrees above zero but so still it did n't seem cold. There has been a good deal of snow, and the streets are very slippery. It is impossible to walk at all without goloshes.

"Mr. Jayne went after dinner to a meeting of a philosophical society founded by Franklin. He brought back philosophers and learned men of all sorts. We talked on astronomy. I told them I had once walked down the tube of Lord Rosse's big telescope. Mr. Jayne told of Herschel having his telescope brought to him when he was old that he might look at Orion and remember it as his last view of the heavens.

"The Jaynes and some of the philosophers went on to a ball at the Assembly Rooms, and I was invited. It gave me a sense of Philadelphia being a community of its own—very entertaining.

"A Rev. John —— called on me yesterday, sending in a message that I used to teach him his catechism at Killinane Church. I had forgotten, but remembered him as a little Protestant boy. Something made me ask what church he belonged to. 'Catholic.' I said: 'My catechism did n't do much good then?' 'Yes,' he said, 'I was an Anglican clergyman for a great many years.' 'Why did you change?' 'Because of authority. I wanted authority, and I cannot give up the belief in the divinity of our dear Lord.' 'But we believe that.' 'No, it 's being given up little by little, and the bishops seemed uncertain. I wanted authority.'

"When we parted we talked about Roxborough thirty-eight years ago. I said, 'We must say a little prayer now and again for each other.' He said, 'Will you please say a great many for me.'

"By orders from New York two secret service men were sent to see me safely home from the theatre, quite unnecessary for Mr. Jayne, who is a leading lawyer, was sufficient escort."

"January 16th. We had a little trouble last night, the first of *The Playboy*. The first act had n't gone far when a man got up and protested loudly and would n't stop. Others shouted to him to go out or keep quiet, and called out 'New York Irish,' but it was a good while before the police could be stirred up to remove him. By that time another man in the stalls was calling out 'This is an insult.' The men near were calling to him to clear out, but they did n't help to evict him. It was Robinson who came at last and led him out like a lamb, but I believe he made some disturbance in the hall. By this time others had started a demonstration in the balcony and there was a good deal of noise, so that for about ten minutes the play could n't be heard. I went round, but did n't make the actors repeat it, for I thought the audience ought to be made to suffer for not being more helpful. About twenty-five men were ejected or walked out, but all were given back their money at the box office, and I am sure will think it a sacred duty to spend it in the same way again. Two were arrested for assault. Nothing was thrown but a slice of currant cake, which hit Sinclair, and two or three eggs, which missed him—he says they were fresh ones. I lectured at the University this afternoon; some of the students had come and invited me. A very fine attendance, many of the audience standing. I spoke only half an hour, but made quite a new little lecture and it held them. I gave eight tickets to be given to athletes among the Pennsylvania students as A. D. C.'s for me to-night. They would have been very useful putting out offenders and taking messages to the stage. I rehearsed this morning, and then lectured and went to a 'College Club' tea—and I am tired and won't write more."

"January 17th. The riot last night was not so serious as I had expected. The agitators had been so gently dealt with the first night and had had their money returned, one felt sure they would try again, and when I got to the theatre, one of the officials told me he had been watching the box office during the day, and had seen 'murderers' taking four or five seats together. The auditorium was very full, and at the back, where I sat, there were a great many suspicious-looking characters. One of them began to cough loudly during *Kathleen ni Houlihan* when Miss Allgood was singing the first little song, and to mutter, so that people near told him he was not the only person in the theatre. Others joined in coughing, bnt I sent a message round to have the lights put up, and the moment they were turned on, the coughs stopped. I pointed out this man, and was amused to see him sit through the play looking sullen but silent except for an occasional mutter or cough, which was stopped at once, for a policeman in plain clothes had been put on each side of him. Near the end, where all on the stage rush out after Christy when he is going to 'kill his father the second time,' he could not resist laughing, and then he walked out discomfited.

"There was a man behind me who coughed

loudly at intervals all through and sounded as if making ready to spit, so that it took all my courage not to move. In the third act, when Christy boasts of having 'cleft his father to the breeches belt,' he called out 'Shame, shame!' several times and walked out. However, whether he repented or looked through the glass screen at back of the stalls and saw the father come to life again, I don't know, but he returned and stayed to the end.

"The first man who made a noise was the most difficult to deal with. He crooked his legs round the legs of his chair, and it took four men to take him out. One, with a large roll of paper in his hand, stood up and called out that he represented the County Down. There were fifteen evicted altogether, all from the stalls, and some others walked out shouting protests.

"The police were more energetic last night and did their work very well and with joy, as Irish policemen would. The inspector too was there and seemed very determined. Also, I had my eight young athletes from the University at hand, ready and willing to give aid. The play was not interrupted for more than a minute or two at a time. I told the players to stop speaking whenever there was a row, and to resume when it was over, so nothing was really lost. A good half of the protesters last night stayed till the end of the play. I think they were waiting for the bad bits to begin, so they saw it at all events. The papers say snuff was thrown, but I think not. I think it was premeditated coughing, but the throats did n't hold out very long. On the other hand, there were a lot of rough-looking Irishmen near me, three together on my bench,who did not take any part in the disturbance, and seemed to enjoy the play. I am sure, therefore, that there will be two parties. . . . I am having my University boys again to-night. Flynn had to leave in the middle of the evening and Robinson took Mrs. Flynn to the opera, so we were a little short-handed, but got on all right. John Quinn is coming from New York and will stay the night, so I shall be quite easy."

"January 17th. At two o'clock I was just finishing lunch alone, Mrs. Jayne lunching out and Mr. Jayne being in bed with a cold, when I was rung up by Mr. Bradford, our manager at the Adelphi, to say that he had warning from Lieblers that we might have to change the bill to-night and take off *The Playboy.* I said that could not be done, but he said it might be necessary. There is some legal point, and Mr. Bradford thought that we might all be arrested if we went on. I said I would rather be arrested than withdraw the play and could answer for the players feeling the same. He said there was also danger that Shubert, to whom the theatre belongs, might close it. I said that would be bad but not so bad as withdrawing *The Playboy,* for it would be Shubert's doing not ours, though that might not be much help in the public view. I was anxious, and I told Bradford not to consent to anything without consulting me. Then I called up John Quinn at New York, got him at his office, and asked him to see the Lieblers, and said that I need not tell him I would sooner go to my death than give in. He said he would see them at once, and that he would be here this evening, as he had intended. At 4 o'clock I heard again from Bradford. He said it had been decided to go on, and that a bail bond had been prepared. He asked if there was anyone to represent me in case of my arrest. I said I would wait to consult

Quinn. It is such a mercy he is coming. My only fear is lest they should get out an injunction to stop the matinée to-morrow; even that would be claimed as a victory. They had told me at the theatre this morning there would probably be trouble to-night. The men arrested were let out, had their money returned, and were escorted through the streets by an admiring crowd. However, I should like to avoid arrest, because of the publicity; one would feel like a suffragette."

"Thursday, 18th. When Quinn arrived, we went straight to the theatre—it was then 7:15—and found the whole cast had already been technically arrested! The tactics of the enemy had been to arrest them in the theatre at 8 o'clock and so make a performance impossible. But the theatre lawyer had managed to circumvent them, and the Chief of Police, now our warm friend, had said he would not only refuse to let his men arrest the actors, but he would have anyone arrested who came on the stage to do so. In the end the warrants of arrest were issued and the manager of the theatre signed bail bonds for the appearance of the Company on Friday morning. The warrants are founded on a bill passed last year in the municipality before S. Bernhardt's visit, forbidding 'immoral or indecent plays.' Our accuser is a liquor dealer. I should have been completely bewildered by the whole thing, but Quinn seemed to unravel it. We had a consultation with the theatre lawyer, and Mr. Jayne's partners, Mr. Biddle and Mr. Yocum, to whom he had sent me. The question seems to be whether it is best to have the hearing put off and brought before a judge, or whether to have it settled straight off to-morrow. The danger is that our case may come up for trial after some weeks, bringing us back here, making it possible for the enemy to boast that we were under bail. Quinn is this morning seeing all the lawyers again, and some decision as to our course will be come to.

"The Commissioner of Public Safety attended the play last night, and said the attack on it must be a joke. . . . I have been interrupted in this by the correspondent of the *Telegraph* coming to ask if it is true, as stated by the Irish Societies, that I am an envoy of the English Government. I referred him to Mr. Bryce, who, I suppose, would be my paymaster!"

"Saturday, 20th. I have been too anxious

and hard worked to write since Thursday. That was the last performance of *The Playboy*, and there was an immense audience. I could not get a seat. Even the little boxes at the top—it is a very high theatre with eight boxes at each side—were all taken. I had made appointments with reporters and others, and had to get a high stool from the office put in the passage and sit there or at the back of the stage. It was the record matinée of the Adelphi. There was tremendous enthusiasm and not a sign of any disturbance. Of course, we had a good many policemen in the house, to the great regret of the management, who had to turn so much good money away. So that was quite a cheerful day. Someone in the audience was heard declaring that the players are not Irish, but all Jews. I had an anonymous letter from some one, who accuses me of the usual crimes and winds up: 'The writer has never saw the play, but has read all about you and it'! That is the way with most of the letter writers, I think.

"Yesterday, Friday morning, we attended the Magistrate's Court at nine o'clock. We had to wait nearly an hour in a tiny, stuffy room. When the hearing began, I was given a chair behind the Magistrate, but the others had either to sit at the back of the inner room, where they could not see or hear, or stand as they did, for over an hour. The liquor-seller, our prosecutor, was the first witness. He had stayed only till Shawneen's 'coat of a Christian man' was left in Michael James's hands. He made a disturbance then and was turned out, but was able to find as much indecency even in that conversation as would demoralise a monastery. His brother, a priest, had stayed all through, and found we had committed every sin mentioned in the Act. Another witness swore that sentences were used in the play and that he had heard them, though they are not either in book nor play. Several witnesses were examined or asked to speak, all giving the same story, 'or if it was not the same story, anyway it was no less than the first story.'

"Our actors were furious. Kerrigan tried hard to keep from breaking out and risking all when the priest was attacking his (that is Shawn Keogh's) character and intentions. At last he called out, 'My God!' and the Magistrate said, 'If that man interrupts the Court again, turn him out,' forgetting that he was speaking of a prisoner at the bar! Indeed, as the prosecutors grew excited, the trial of the Irish Players seemed to be forgotten, and it became the trial of Christy Mahon for the attempted murder of his father. Mr. Gray demanded that the actors should be 'held for Court,' but Quinn, knowing what would happen, had arranged for this, and our lawyers 'sued out a writ of *habeas corpus*' (I hope this is the right expression) and had arranged with Judge Carr to try the case in the afternoon. Mr. Gray wanted then to have it tried at once. He said he had to leave town in the afternoon, but in the end the Judge said he could not arrange for the trial before three o'clock. This gave me time to telephone to John Quinn, who had thought the trial was not to be till next morning, and was attending cases of his own in New York. He answered that he would come if he possibly could. Then there was a message that he had missed the train by one minute, but had caught another, ten minutes later. At three o'clock we went to the Court, a large one this time. The Judge did n't know anything about the play, and had to be told the whole story as it went on, just like old Wall in Dublin at our first riot, so before the case had gone far audience and officials were in a broad grin. The liquor-dealer got a different hearing this time, was asked some pertinent questions instead of being simply encouraged, as he was by the Magistrate.

"The dramatic event was the arrival of Quinn while a witness was being examined. We had got leave from the Judge for him to cross-examine, and the witness had to confess that the people of Ireland do use the name of God at other times than in blessing or thanking those who have been kind to them, and in gratitude or prayer, as he had at first asserted upon oath. Also when he based his attack on indecency by quoting the 'poacher's love,' spoken of by Christy, he was made to admit that, a few sentences earlier, marriage had been spoken of, 'in a fortnight's time when the banns will be called.' Whether this made it more or less moral, he was not asked to say. He called the play 'libidinous.'

"J. Q. asked one witness if anything immoral had happened on the stage, and he answered 'Not while the curtain was up!' I think it was the same witness who said, 'A theatre is no place for a sense of humour.' The players beamed and the audience enjoyed themselves, and then when the Director of Public Safety was called and said he and his wife had enjoyed the play very much and had seen nothing to shock anybody, the enemy had received, as Quinn said, 'a knock-out blow.' He made a very fine speech then. There is just a little bit of it in the *North American*, but Mr. Gray made objections to its being reported, but anyhow, it turned the tables completely on the enemy. It was a little disappointment that the Judge did not give his verdict there and then, that we might have cabled home.

"A lot of people have been expressing sympathy. A young man from the University, who had been bringing a bodyguard for me on the riot nights, has just been to say good-bye, and told me the students are going to hold an indignation meeting. The Drama League, six hundred strong, has so far done or said nothing, though it is supposed to have sent out a bulletin endorsing the favourable opinion of Boston upon our plays, a week after we came here, not having had time to form an opinion of its own. Can you imagine their allowing such a thing to happen here as the arrest of a company of artists engaged in producing a masterpiece, and at such hands! The Administration has been re-formed of late and is certainly on the mend, but there is plenty more to be done, although the city has an innocent look, as if it had gone astray in the fields, and its streets are named after trees. The Company are in a state of fury, but they adore John Quinn, and his name will pass into folk-lore like those stories of O'Connell suddenly appearing at trials. He spoke splendidly, with fire and full knowledge. You will see what he said about the witnesses in the *North American* and even Robinson says he 'came like an angel.'

"Sunday, 21st. Yesterday was a little depressing, for the Judge had not yet given out his decision; so we are still under bail and the imputations of indecency, etc. The Philadelphians say it is because the Act is such a new one, it requires a great deal of consideration.

"A reporter came yesterday to ask whether I considered *The Playboy* immoral. I said my taking it about was answer enough, but that if he wished to give interesting news, he would go to the twenty-six witnesses produced against us (we were not allowed to produce one on our side) and try to get at their opinions, and on what they were founded. He answered that he had already been to ten of them that morning, that they all answered in the same words, not two words of difference—that their opinion was founded on the boy and the girl being left alone in the house for the night. They can hardly have heard Quinn making the clerical witness withdraw his statement that immorality was implied by their being left together. I advised him also to look at the signed articles on the play in so many English and American magazines, and to remember that even here the plays have been taught in the dramatic classes of the University of Pennsylvania, that the President of Bryn Mawr had invited the players to the College for the day, and had sent a large party of students to the last matinée of *The Playboy*, leave being asked to introduce them to me. I told him he might print all this opposite the witnesses' opinions.

"Yesterday's matinée, *Rising of the Moon*, *Well of the Saints*, and *Workhouse Ward*, was again so crowded that I could not get a place and went and sat in the side-wings, where a cinematograph man came to ask if I would allow *The Playboy* to be used for a moving-picture exhibition, as it would be 'such a good advertisement for us!' Last night also there was a very good audience. We took just one dollar short of eight thousand dollars in the week. Such a pity the dollars were returned to the disturbers or we should have gone above it."

"I was advised to go to a certain newspaper office to get evidence that was considered necessary as to the standing of the magistrate who had issued the writ and before whom we had been brought (we had been advised to take an action for malicious arrest). The editor was generous enough to let me have from the files, classified in the newspaper office as 'Obituary Notices,' ready for use at the proper time an envelope containing reports of some curious incidents in the record of the magistrate in question. The editor lamented his troubles of the evening before when he had gone for supper to the Bellevue where I had met him. He had taken to the restaurant a young niece, who wanted something delicate for supper, whereas the editor himself wanted two soft-boiled eggs with rice and cream. These simple dishes, however, could not be had at the fashionable Bellevue and he was able but to pick at a little of the delicate food. After he had taken the niece home, he made off to his own little homely restaurant, where he secured his rice and eggs. This, and an interview I had seen with Yeats, who supposes that our arrest was due to the fact that Philadelphia is a Puritan town, brought back the rural atmosphere."

Our friends at home were naturally amazed, especially in London where the posters of the newspapers had in large letters, "ARREST OF THE IRISH PLAYERS." Mr. Yeats wrote from Dublin, January 21st: "I need not tell you how startled I was when a reporter came to me on Thursday evening and asked me whether I had anything to say regarding the arrest of the Abbey Players. While I was talking to him and telling him I did n't really know anything about it (he was as ignorant of your crime as I was), a second reporter came in, equally urgent and ignorant. Then a wire came from the London correspondent of the *New York Sun*, asking for an opinion on the arrest of Abbey Players. We were speculating as to what it could mean, and I was surmising it was *Blanco*, when a telegram came from the *Manchester Guardian*, saying it was *The Playboy* and asking me to see their reporter. Then a young man arrived with a telegram, and I thought he was the reporter and became very eloquent. He was sympathetic and interested, and when I had finished, explained that he was only the post-office messenger. Then another reporter turned up and after that the *Manchester Guardian* man. You will have had the papers before this. I think for the moment it has made us rather popular here in Dublin, for no matter how much evil people wish for the Directors, they feel amiable towards the players. If only Miss Allgood could get a fortnight, I think the pit would love even *The Playboy*. However, I imagine that after a few days of the correspondence columns, we shall discover our enemies again.

"We have done very well this week with the school. I am rather anxious that the school, or No. 2 Company, as it will be, should have in its repertory some of our most popular pieces. . . . The great thing achieved is that if Philadelphia had permanently imprisoned the whole Company, our new Company would in twelve months have taken their place here in Dublin. We have now a fine general effect, though we have no big personalities."

"Philadelphia, Monday. I forget what I have written, and I don't know if I have explained that we were allowed no witnesses, either at the Magistrate's or the Judge's Court, and with our hastily instructed lawyers we should not have been able to make even any defence through them but for the miraculous appearance of John Quinn. And this is the fifth day we have been under bail on charge of indecency, and its like."

"January 22d, Hotel Algonquin, New York. Contrary to my directions Liebler's man had put on *The Playboy* for Pittsburg. It was asked for by some ladies who are taking the whole house for a charity performance. Now they have written to ask for another bill instead, *Hyacinth*, *Riders*, *Workhouse;* and the papers say that *The Playboy* has been taken off on religious grounds."

"Richmond, Indiana, January 24th. The journey to Pittsburg is a quite lovely journey, like Switzerland but less monotonous; the sunshine and snow exhilarating. The plays had begun when I arrived. There was a very good audience and *Hyacinth* and *Workhouse Ward* made them laugh a great deal. Carnegie Hall is all gilding and marbles, and a gilded organ towers above the butcher's shop in *Hyacinth*. I had to make a little speech and was able to tell of the telegram from Philadelphia, saying the Judge had dismissed the case. We came on here through the night.

"An interviewer who came this morning has sent me an interesting book on Indiana book plates, and an old lady brought me an Irish Bible, and the jeweller who packed my watch would take nothing, and Miss Allgood has sent me a box of roses. So the stars must be in a good mood. I think we ought to start with *The Playboy* in Chicago and get that over. It would show we are not damped by Philadelphia."

We went on that night to Indianapolis. *The Playboy* had been specially asked for in Indianapolis. Protests against its production were made to the manager of the theatre by the Ancient Order of Hibernians and others, but the manager said he was powerless. They also called upon Superintendent of Police Hyland, who said: "I will have plenty of men at the theatre to quell a disturbance. I don't believe, however, that there will be any trouble. If there are persons who do not like the show, they can stay away. But there is one thing certain; if they do not stay away and come to the show to make trouble, they will find plenty of it on hand."

The Mayor was also appealed to, but he did not see his way to stop the play. The Irish Societies then decided to stay away, and though the theatre was packed, the play went through in perfect peace.

"Chicago, Hotel La Salle, January 26th. Tyler wired me to come on here, so I left the Company at Indianapolis this morning and came on. We don't begin playing here till the 5th. No theatre is ready. Gaston Mayer was very urgent we should stay another week on account of getting here so late. I told the Company of this and they decided to stay. We shall therefore finish here March 2d and sail on the 6th. We had no trouble at Indianapolis last night. The police authorities were very firm and the threats collapsed. I wish Philadelphia had been as firm. They are all afraid of the politicians. . . .

"I was sorry to leave the Company. I feel

like Wilhelm Meister going through ever-fresh adventures with the little troop. As to the rows, I don't think there is anything you (Yeats) could have done, except that you would have done things yourself while others have done them for me. The Company insist on giving John Quinn a silver cup, in gratitude for his help. I have n't seen Flynn for a fortnight. He is astray among the one-night towns and talked to us at Indianapolis through the telephone, with a bad cold."

"25th or 26th. I see by the papers that at the La Salle Hotel, where I am staying, a meeting of Irishmen has been held at which an 'Anti-Irish Players' League' was formed, beginning with a membership of three hundred. Such a pity I could n't have slipped in to the meeting! A petition had also been written and was being sent out for signature, demanding the suppression of *The Playboy*. This petition was said to have been signed by eight thousand persons, and twenty thousand signatures were expected. Meanwhile the Anti-Cruelty Society of Chicago, at the head of which are various benevolent ladies, had asked leave to buy up the whole house for the first performance of *The Playboy of the Western World.* They meant to resell these seats at an increased price for their charity and believed it was likely to draw the largest audience. So they have taken the theatre for Tuesday, February 6, and the public performance of *The Playboy* will take place the next day."

"January 29th. My typewriter is mended at last, and I am getting settled. Last night one of the boy interviewers—they are all boys here—came in from one of the papers. He showed me two statements written by Liebler's manager here, one colourless, the other offering a reward of five thousand dollars to anyone who could prove the management had bribed rioters for the first night, as has been stated in the papers. I advised that this be put in, as people really seem to believe it is true. This young man had been to see many of the objectors. They said Synge was a 'degenerate,' who had lived abroad to collect a bad atmosphere, which he put round Irish characters afterwards. A nice young interviewer; he wants to write a play around his mother's life, to show what a mother's devotion can be. Another of them is twenty-five and is going to be married next summer. He showed me his fiancée's portrait, and another went and hunted for a Don Quixote I wanted, to distract my mind from present-day things.

"This morning one came who is in with the Irish Clubs and had all the objections, but now seems quite friendly. He says one of the chief officers of the 'Anti-Irish Players' League' is a man called H., a son of old Mrs. H.! He has hinted that my sympathies are with the landlord side, and that he could tell tales of hard treatment. The interviewer wanted to know if a rehearsal could be held for the Mayor so that he might judge the play, but I said the first night under the patronage of the Anti-Cruelty Society would give him his opportunity. A lady interviewer then came, but I made her take her pencil and write down what I did say, which is more than the boys do. I tell them I put in my pig and it comes out sausage."

"Tuesday, January 30th. I am so tired! Last night I dined with the Hamills, friends of John Quinn. It was a very pleasant dinner and we all went afterwards to see *The Woman*, a good play in its realistic way. I came home quite cheery but found in the passage one of my young interviewers, who told me the Town Council had unanimously voted against *The Playboy* being put on. He had been sent to ask me for a statement, but advised me not to make one, and there was nothing to say. I was going to bed near midnight when another interviewer arrived, and said the Mayor had acted on the recommendation of the Council and suppressed the play. He showed me an article which was to appear in the morning issue of his paper telling this. I was very sad for it seemed as if there was an end of the fight. The hot water-apparatus in my room, which is always out of order, began grunting and groaning between one and two when I was asleep and wakened me; so I got no more sleep till late morning, and then was awaked by interviewers at the telephone. They even knocked at my door while I was dressing.

"When I went down, however, I found that the Mayor had not ordered the play off, and the article in the paper had had to be re-printed. Also Flynn arrived and was a help with the army who came in, entertaining them while I typed out a statement about the adventures of *The Playboy* so far, and this statement I gave them. Then I 'phoned to Mr. Hamill, who is a lawyer and who had said last night he would help me in any legal difficulty. He came at once and was splendid. He went into the law of the case, and believes that if the Mayor does forbid it, we can take him into the Federal Court, and go on all right. He says another lawyer, who was at dinner last night, has also volunteered to serve. He went to try and see the Mayor but missed him. He is, however, to see him at noon to-morrow. He came back at five for another talk, and says he does n't think the Mayor has power to stop it. He has seen the Corporation lawyer.

"I was engaged to lunch with a nice Mrs.—— at one, but got there after the hour and had to be back here before two, and it was an absurd thing: I had had my room changed. I had suffered so much from the unmanageable hot water that I threatened the manager that I would tell the interviewers about it, and he at once gave me another suite. My things were being brought up, and I could n't find hat or coat, therefore had to go just as I was. However the lunch was very pleasant and good, what I had of it. . . .

"I came back to find a Mr. Field, editor of one of the papers, who had brought 'an enemy,' who announced he had come but for five minutes to hear my views, and spent at least ten in giving his own. Then Liebler's local manager came in. He also thinks we shall be able to circumvent the Mayor. He believes, however, the Mayor will give the order for political reasons, though he has some culture and would not like to be classed with the Aldermen. A couple of ladies called. One comfort of being attacked is that one finds friends to help. . . .

"I have nice rooms now on the ninth floor—there are twenty-two floors altogether—the place riddled with telephones, radiators, etc. I was glad to hear the voice of a fat housemaid from Mayo a while ago.

"It is a strange fate that sends me into battle after my peaceful life for so many years, and especially over *Playboy*, that I have never really loved, but one has to carry through one's job. One of the accusations has been that there are no Irish persons connected with the Company, and my answer is given accurately in one of the papers. 'The Players are all Irish by birth. They had never left Ireland until they came to England on the tours made by us. With two exceptions all are Roman Catholics.

"'I believe the play is quite honestly considered by some of my countrymen out here to be injurious to Ireland and her claim for self-government, but I know that such an assumption is wrong and that the dignity of Ireland has been very much increased by the work of the Theatre, of which the genius of Mr. Synge is a component part.'"

"February 1st. Yesterday morning I took a holiday, went to see a little amateur play in a private house. It was on suffrage, called *Every-woman*, very short and rather amusing. It was given at 11 o'clock and afterwards there was an 'informal lunch,' rather a good idea,—little tables, not set out, here and there. There were first cups of delicious soup, then vegetable sandwiches with little cases of hot mince, and peas, just a plate and fork, then ices and black coffee, and bonbons. It was much pleasanter than sitting down to a table; one could move about. The luncheon was all over by 1:30, and then a Mrs. R—— took me for a drive in her motor. We drove about thirty miles about the park and town and along the lake side, but never really away from the town, which is immense. The lake is lovely, a soft turquoise blue, not the blue of the sea, and there was floating ice near the shore. It was luckily a bright day, the first we have had. To-day there is snow again and darkness.

"When I came home, I set to work to correct a copy of *The Playboy* according to the prompt copy I had just had sent on by the Company, in case the Mayor wanted it. A journalist came in who wanted to know about the cuts, and I got him to help me. Then Mr. Hamill came; he does n't think there will be trouble. Then I took up a lot of telephone addresses that had been left for me to call up, and found one was from 'W. Dillon.' It was a Mr. Dillon representing the enemy, who had been brought to see me on Tuesday. My interview with him had appeared in a very mangled form next day and I found only then that he was a brother of John Dillon, M.P., and the Corporation lawyer. I called him up, and he answered from the City Hall, and said he was writing a report on the legal aspect of the case for the Mayor, and wanted to know if I was sure certain words had been left out of the acting version, as I told him had always been done. I said yes, and I could now bring him the prompt copy. He assented and I went round to the City Hall. Mr. Dillon was sitting in his office, dictating to a shorthand writer. He said, 'You may listen to what I am dictating, but you must treat it as confidential.' I said, 'I will go away if you wish,' but he said, 'No, I will trust to your honour as a lady.' He was just finishing his statement, as printed in the papers this morning, denouncing the play but saying that, though in his opinion it might lead to a riot, he did not think the Mayor had power to stop it. I showed him the prompt copy. He asked if we could not strike out still more. I said the passages we had changed or left out had been changed in Mr. Synge's lifetime and with his consent, and we did not feel justified in meddling any more. I think he expected me to make some concession, for he said then, 'I think you would do much better to take the play off altogether.' I said we were bound by contract to Liebler to put on whatever plays they asked for. He said, 'Then it is not in your power to remove it?' I answered, 'No,' and that ended the matter. I felt sorry for the moment, for it would have been gracious to make some small concession, but afterwards I thought of Parnell. . . . We may bring that play some other time, and there are many who think his betrayal a greater slur upon Ireland than would be even the real killing of a father.

"The *Examiner* announces that the Mayor won't stop the play. He has said. 'I do not see how the performance can be stopped. I have read part of it and its chief characteristic seems to be stupidity rather than immorality. I should think it would take more than a regiment of soldiers to compel an audience to fill the Grand Opera House to see such a poor production. I certainly shall not see it.'

"I hope I may get some breathing time. The idea of a day spent playing with little Richard seems an impossible heaven! And I feel a little lonely at times. It is a mercy this will be the last fight. I don't think it is over yet. . . . I like to hear of the success of the school. It will be a great enjoyment sitting down to listen to a verse play again if I survive to do it!"

"Feb. 3rd. I dined with the McC——s, and went on to the Opera, *Tristan und Isolde*, which

I had never seen. It was a great delight, a change from worries. I like the people here. They are more merry than those of the other cities somehow, at least those I have fallen amongst. They are vital. They don't want to die till they see what Chicago is going to do.

"There is snow on the ground and yesterday when I went for a walk, the cold frightened me at first,—such pain in the face, but I went on and got used to it. The thermometer has been six below zero."

"Feb. 8th. I seem to have been busy ever since. The first night of *The Playboy* was anxious. I was not really anxious the Anti-Cruelty night, and it went off quite peaceably, but I was last night, the open one, for, as I quoted from *Image*, 'There are always contrary people in a crowd.' But the play was acted in entire peace. I nearly fell asleep! It seems complete victory. The Corporation had to rescind their resolution against it, and I suppose the objectors found public opinion was too strong to permit any protest to be made. It is a great mercy. I did not know how great the strain was till it was over.

"On Monday we opened to a fairly large house

with comedies and they were well received. The Hull House Players came and gave me a lovely bunch of roses. They have been acting some of my plays. When I got back to the hotel, I found a threatening letter written in vile language, and with picture of coffin and pistol, saying I would 'never see the hills of Connemara again,' and was about to meet with my death. It seems a miracle to have got through such a Wood of Dangers with flags flying."

"Feb. 12th. Everything goes on so peaceably we are astonished. *The Playboy* finished its five days' run on Saturday with never a boo or a hiss. I believe the enemy are making some excuse for themselves, saying they won't riot because it was said they were paid to do so, but it is an extraordinary defeat for them. Quinn was much excited over it when he was here, and he did not know the extent of our victory. He thinks it the pricking of the bubble of all the societies that have been terrorising people. Fibs go on, of course, and a Mrs. F—— told me that her Irish maid said she had been forbidden to go to *The Playboy* 'because it runs down the courage of the Irish.' She was sad, and said 'The Irish always had courage.'

"It makes one think *The Playboy* more harmless even than one had thought, their having to make up these inventions. One is glad to put it on for them to see. I feel like Pegeen showing off Christy to the Widow Quinn, 'See now is he roaring, romping?' The author of 'An Open Letter to Lady Gregory' came to me at some Club to ask if I had seen it. I said yes, and that the paper had telephoned to know if I would answer it, but I had said no, and that I wished all my critics would write me open letters instead of personal ones, as I could leave them unanswered without discourtesy.

"We have a good following among the intellectuals, and a good many Irish begin to come in. We know that by the reception of *Rising of the Moon.*

"Coming back from my lecture at Detroit, I was to have arrived at Chicago at eight o'clock. I awoke to find we were in a blizzard. The train got stuck in a suburb of Chicago, and after hours of waiting we had to wade across the track, ankle deep in snow, I in my thin shoes! After fighting the blizzard, we had to sit in a shed for another hour or two. Then they said we must wade back to the train. They thought it could be run to the station. I thought I might as well wait for my end where I was, as I could not carry my baggage and there was no one to help me, so stayed on my bench. After a bit some omnibuses came to our relief, and I being near the door was put in first, and got to the hotel at three o'clock. I had not had breakfast, expecting we should be in, and when I asked for it later, the car had been taken off, so all the food I had was a dry roll I had taken from the hotel on Sunday. However, I was none the worse, and glad to have seen a blizzard. It was the worst they had had for many years, deaths were caused by it, and much damage was done.

"I have been walking to the theatre every night as usual in spite of that threatening letter. I don't feel anxious, for I don't think from the drawing that the sender has much practical knowledge of firearms.

"I can hardly believe we shall sail next week! It will be a great rest surely. . . Well, we have had a great victory!"

THE BINDING

I HAD but just written these pages and put together these letters when in last Christmas week we set out again for America. We spent there the first four months of this year, but this time there were no riots and we were of the happy people who have no history, unless it may be of the continued kindness of America, and of the growing kindness and better understanding on the part of our own countrymen

Last year, it was often said to me in New York and elsewhere, "You must not think that we Americans helped in these attacks." And I would answer, "No; our countrymen took care to make that clear by throwing our national potato. If you had attacked us you would have thrown pumpkins, and we should have fared worse than Æsop's philosopher under the oak."

I think the facts I have given show that the opposition was in every case planned and ordered before the plays had been seen—before we landed, and by a very small group working through a political organisation. As to the reason and meaning of that attack, it is for those who made it to set that out. I cannot but remember Alexander Hamilton's words when the building of America began: "After this war is over, will come the real war, the great battle of ideas"; and that the long political war in Ireland may be, and seems to be, nearing its end. I think too of Laeg looking out from the wounded Cuchulain's tent and making his report at Ilgaireth: "I see a little herd of cattle breaking out from the west of Ailell's camp, and there are lads following after them and trying to bring them back, and I see more lads coming out from the army of Ulster to attack them"; and how Cuchulain said: "That little herd on the plain is the beginning of a great battle." The battle of ideas has been fought elsewhere and against other dramatists. Was not Ibsen banished from his country, and Molière refused Christian burial?

It is after all the old story of the two sides of the shield. Some who are lovers of Ireland believe we have lessened the dignity of Ireland by showing upon the stage countrymen who drink and swear and admire deeds of violence, or who are misers and covetous or hungering after land. We who are lovers of Ireland believe that our Theatre with its whole mass of plays has very greatly increased that dignity, and we are content to leave that judgment to the great arbitrator, Time. And amongst the Irish in America it was easy to rouse feeling against us. Is not the new baby always the disturber in the household? Our school of drama is the newest birth in Ireland, that Ireland which had become almost consecrated by distance and by romance. An old Irishwoman who loves her country very much said while I was in America: "I don't want to go back and see Ireland again. It is a finished picture in my mind." But Ireland cannot always be kept as a sampler upon the wall. It has refused to be cut off from the creative work of the intellect, and the other countries creating literature have claimed her as of their kin.

I wish my countrymen, before coming into the fight, had known it to be so unequal. They had banished from the stage one or two plays that had given them offence and no one had greatly cared. But works of imagination such as those of Synge could not be suppressed even if burned in the market place. They had not realised the tremendous support we had, that we were not fighting alone, but with the intellect of America as well as of Europe at our back.

There was another thing they had not reckoned with. It had been put down in words by Professor William James: "Democracy is still upon its trial. The civic genius of our people is its only bulwark and neither laws nor monuments, neither battleships nor public libraries, nor churches nor universities can save us from degeneration if the inner mystery be lost. That mystery, at once the secret and glory of our English-speaking race, consists in nothing but two common habits, two inveterate habits, carried into public life. One of these is the habit of trained and disciplined good temper towards the opposite party when it fairly wins its innings. The other is that of fierce and merciless resentment towards every man or set of men who break the public peace."

The civic genius of America decided that not we but our opponents had broken the public peace.

Now, little Richard, that is the whole story of my journey; and I wonder if by the time you can read it you will have forgotten my coming home with a big basket of grapes and bananas and grapefruit and oranges for you, and a little flag with the Stars and Stripes.

I was very glad to be at home with you again while the daffodils were blooming out, and to have no more fighting, perhaps for ever. And if it is hard to fight for a thing you love, it is harder to fight for one you have no great love for. And you will read some day in one of those books in the library that are too high now for you to reach, the story of a man who was said to be mad but has outlived many who were not, and who went about fighting for the sake of some one who was maybe "the fright of seven townlands with her biting tongue" though he still called out after every battle, "Dulcinea is the most beautiful woman of the world!" So think a long time before you choose your road, little Richard, but when you have chosen it, follow it on to the end.

COOLE, July 24, 1913.

Appendices

APPENDIX I

PLAYS PRODUCED BY THE ABBEY THEATRE CO. AND ITS PREDECESSORS, WITH DATES OF FIRST PERFORMANCES

IRISH LITERARY THEATRE AT ANTIENT CONCERT ROOMS

May 8th, 1899.	"The Countess Cathleen."	W. B. Yeats
" 9th, "	"The Heather Field."	Edward Martyn

IRISH LITERARY THEATRE AT THE GAIETY THEATRE

Feb. 19th, 1900.	"The Bending of the Bough."	George Moore
" 19th, "	"The Last Feast of the Fianna."	Alice Milligan
" 20th, "	"Maeve."	Edward Martyn
Oct. 21st, 1901.	"Diarmuid and Grania."	W. B. Yeats and George Moore
" 21st, "	"The Twisting of the Rope."	Douglas Hyde

(The first Gaelic Play produced in any Theatre.)

MR. W. G. FAY'S IRISH NATIONAL DRAMATIC COMPANY AT ST. TERESA'S HALL, CLARENDON STREET.

Apr. 2nd, 1902.	"Deirdre."	"A.E."
" 2nd, "	"Kathleen Ni Houlihan."	W. B. Yeats.

IRISH NATIONAL DRAMATIC COMPANY AT ANTIENT CONCERT ROOMS

Oct. 29th, 1902.	"The Sleep of the King."	Seumas O'Cuisin

Oct. 29th, 1902.	"The Laying of the Foundations."	Fred Ryan
" 30th, "	"A Pot of Broth."	W. B. Yeats
" 31st, "	"The Racing Lug."	Seumas O'Cuisin

IRISH NATIONAL THEATRE SOCIETY, MOLESWORTH HALL

(The first prospectus of this Society, dated March, 1903, and signed by Mr. Fred Ryan began as follows: "The Irish National Theatre Society was formed to continue on a more permanent basis the work of the Irish Literary Theatre.")

Mar. 14th, 1903.	"The Hour Glass."	W. B. Yeats
" 14th, "	"Twenty-Five."	Lady Gregory
Oct. 8th, "	"The King's Threshold."	W. B. Yeats
" 8th, "	"In the Shadow of the Glen."	J. M. Synge
Dec. 3rd, "	"Broken Soil."	Padraic Colum
Jan. 14th, 1904.	"The Shadowy Waters."	W. B. Yeats
" 14th, "	"The Townland of Tamney."	Seumas McManus
Feb. 25th, "	"Riders to the Sea."	J. M. Synge

IRISH NATIONAL THEATRE SOCIETY AT THE ABBEY THEATRE.

Dec. 27th, 1904.	"On Baile's Strand."	W. B. Yeats
" 27th, "	"Spreading the News."	Lady Gregory
Feb. 4th, 1905.	"The Well of the Saints."	J. M. Synge
Mar. 25th, "	"Kincora."	Lady Gregory
Apr. 25th, "	"The Building Fund."	William Boyle
June 9th, "	"The Land."	Padraic Colum

NATIONAL THEATRE SOCIETY, LTD. (ABBEY COMPANY)

Dec. 9th, 1905.	"The White Cockade."	Lady Gregory
Jan. 20th, 1906.	"The Eloquent Dempsy."	William Boyle
Feb. 19th, "	"Hyacinth Halvey."	Lady Gregory
Oct. 20th, "	"The Gaol Gate."	Lady Gregory
" 20th, "	"The Mineral Workers."	William Boyle
Nov. 24th, "	"Deirdre."	W. B. Yeats
Dec. 8th, "	"The Canavans."	Lady Gregory

Dec. 8th,	1906.	New Version of "The Shadowy Waters."	W. B. Yeats
Jan. 26th,	1907.	"The Playboy of the Western World."	J. M. Synge
Feb. 23rd,	"	"The Jackdaw."	Lady Gregory
Mar. 9th,	"	"The Rising of the Moon."	Lady Gregory
Apr. 1st,	"	"The Eyes of the Blind."	Miss W. M. Letts
Apr. 3rd,	1907.	"The Poorhouse."	Douglas Hyde and Lady Gregory
" 27th,	"	"Fand."	Wilfrid Scawen Blunt
Oct. 3rd,	"	"The Country Dressmaker."	George Fitz-maurice
" 31st,	"	"Dervorgilla."	Lady Gregory
Nov. 21st,	"	"The Unicorn from the Stars."	W. B. Yeats and Lady Gregory
Feb. 13th,	1908.	"The Man who missed the Tide."	W. F. Casey
" 13th,	"	"The Piper."	Norreys Connell
Mar. 10th,	"	"The Piedish."	George Fitz-maurice
Mar. 19th,	"	"The Golden Helmet."	W. B. Yeats
Apr. 20th,	"	"The Workhouse Ward."	Lady Gregory
Oct. 1st,	"	"The Suburban Groove."	W. F. Casey
" 8th,	"	"The Clancy Name."	Lennox Robinson
" 15th,	"	"When the Dawn is come."	Thomas Mac-Donogh
" 21st,	"	New Version, "The Man who missed the Tide."	W. F. Casey
Feb. 11th,	1909.	Revised Version of "Kincora"	Lady Gregory
Mar. 11th,	"	"Stephen Grey."	D. L. Kelleher
Apr. 1st,	"	"The Cross Roads"	Lennox Robinson
" 1st,	"	"Time."	Norreys Connell
" 29th,	"	"The Glittering Gate."	Lord Dunsany

May 27th, "	"An Imaginary Conversation."	Norreys Connell
Aug. 25th, "	"The Shewing-up of Blanco Posnet."	Bernard Shaw
Sept. 16th, "	"The White Feather."	R. J. Ray
Oct. 14th, "	"The Challenge."	Miss W. M. Letts
Nov. 11th, "	"The Image"	Lady Gregory
Jan. 13th, 1910.	"Deirdre of the Sorrows."	J. M. Synge
Feb. 10th, "	"The Green Helmet."	W. B. Yeats
Mar. 2nd, "	"The Travelling Man."	Lady Gregory
May 12th, "	"Thomas Muskerry."	Padraic Colum
" 26th, "	"Harvest."	Lennox Robinson
Sept. 28th, 1910	"The Casting-out of Martin Whelan."	R. J. Ray
Oct. 27th, "	"Birthright."	T. C. Murray
Nov. 10th, "	"The Full Moon."	Lady Gregory
" 24th, "	"The Shuiler's Child."*	Seumas O'Kelly
Dec. 1st, "	"Coats."	Lady Gregory
Jan. 12th, 1911.	"The Deliverer."	Lady Gregory
" 26th, "	"King Argimenes and the Unknown Warrior."	Lord Dunsany
Feb. 16th, "	"The Land of Heart's Desire."†	W. B. Yeats
Mar. 30th, "	"Mixed Marriage."	St. John G. Ervine
Nov. 23rd, "	"The Interlude of Youth."	Anon., first printed 1554
" 23rd, "	"The Second Shepherds' Play."	Anon., *circa* 1400
" 30th, "	"The Marriage."	Douglas Hyde
Dec. 7th, "	"Red Turf."	Rutherford Mayne
" 14th, "	Revival of "The Countess Cathleen."	W. B. Yeats
Jan. 4th, 1912.	"The Annunciation."	*circa* 1400
" 4th, "	"The Flight into Egypt."	*circa* 1400
" 11th, "	"MacDarragh's Wife."	Lady Gregory

* First produced by an amateur company at the Molesworth Hall in 1909.

† First produced at the Avenue Theatre, London, in 1894.

Feb. 1st,	"	Revival of "The Country Dressmaker."	George Fitz-maurice
" 15th,	"	"The Tinker and the Fairy." (Played in Gaelic)	Douglas Hyde
" 29th,	"	"The Worlde and the Chylde."	15th century
Mar. 28th,	"	"Family Failing."	William Boyle
Apr. 11th,	"	"Patriots."	Lennox Robinson
" 15th,	"	"Judgment."	Joseph Campbell
June 20th,	"	"Maurice Harte."	T. C. Murray
July 4th,	"	"The Bogie Men."	Lady Gregory
Oct. 17th,	"	"The Magnanimous Lover."	St. John G. Ervine
Nov. 21st,	"	"Damer's Gold."	Lady Gregory

TRANSLATIONS OF THE FOLLOWING HAVE BEEN PRODUCED

Apr. 16th, 1906.	"The Doctor in spite of Himself."	(Molière.) Translated by Lady Gregory
Mar. 16th, 1907.	"Interior."	(Maeterlinck.)
" 19th, 1908.	"Teja."	(Sudermann.) Translated by Lady Gregory
Apr. 4th, "	"The Rogueries of Scapin."	(Molière.) Translated by Lady Gregory
Jan. 21st, 1909.	"The Miser."	(Molière.) Translated by Lady Gregory
Feb. 24th, 1910.	"Mirandolina."	(Goldoni.) Translated by Lady Gregory.
Jan. 5th, 1911.	"Nativity Play."	(Douglas Hyde.) Translated by Lady Gregory

NEW PRODUCTIONS

Nov. 21st, 1912.	"The Hour Glass" Revised.	
" " "	"Damer's Gold."	
Jan. 23rd, 1913.	"The Dean of St. Patrick's."	G. Sidney Paternoster
Feb. 6th, "	Revival, "Casting-out of Martin Whelan."	R. J. Ray
" 20th, "	"Hannele."	Gerhardt Hauptmann
Mar. 6th, "	"There are Crimes and Crimes."	August Strindberg
" 13th, "	"The Cuckoo's Nest."	John Guinan
Apr. 10th, "	"The Homecoming."	Gertrude Robins
" 17th, "	"The Stronger."	August Strindberg
" 24th, "	"The Magic Glasses."	George Fitzmaurice
" 24th "	"Broken Faith."	S. R. Day and G.D.Cummins
May 17th, "	"The Post Office."	Rabindranath Tagore

APPENDIX II

"THE NATION" ON "BLANCO POSNET"

We have often spoken in these columns of the condition of the British drama and the various ways of mending it. But there is one of its features, or, rather, one of its disabilities, as to which some present decision must clearly be taken. That is the power of the Censorship to warp it for evil, and to maim it for good. There can be no doubt at all that this is the double function of the Lord Chamberlain and his office. The drama that they pass on and therefore commend to the people is a drama that is always earthly, often sensual, and occasionally devilish; the drama which they refuse to the people is a drama that seeks to be truthful, and is therefore not concerned with average sensual views of life, and that might, if it were encouraged, powerfully touch the neglected spheres of morals and religion. As to the first count against the Censorship there is and can be no defence. *Habemus confitentem reum.* The man who would pass *Dear Old Charlie* would pass anything. He has bound himself to tolerate the drama of Wycherley and Congreve, of which it is a fairly exact and clever revival, suited to modern hypocrisy as to ways of expression, but equally audacious in its glorification of lying, adultery, mockery, and light-mindedness.

The case on the other count is, we think, sufficiently made out by the Censor's refusal to license Mr. Bernard Shaw's one-act play, *The Showing-up of Blanco Posnet.* It is fair to the Censor to explain the grounds of his refusal. Mr. Shaw has been good enough to let the editor of this paper see a copy both of his drama and of the official letter refusing a "license for representation" unless certain passages were expunged. There were two such passages. On the second Mr. Shaw assures us that no difficulty could have occurred. It raised a question of taste, on which he was willing to meet Mr. Redford's views. It seems to us outspoken rather than gross, but as it was not the subject of controversy we dismiss it, and recur to the critical point on which Mr. Shaw, considering—and, in our view, rightly considering—that the heart and meaning of his play were at issue, refused to give way. In order that we may explain the quarrel, it is necessary to give some slight sketch of the character and intention of *The Showing-up of Blanco Posnet.* We suggest as the simplest clue to its tone and atmosphere that it reproduces in some measure the subject and the feeling of Bret Harte's *Luck of Roaring Camp.* It depicts a coarse and violent society, governed by emotions and crude wants rather than by principles and laws, a society of drunkards, lynchers, duellists at sight, and, above all, horse-stealers—in other words, a world of conventionally bad men, liable to good impulses. The "hero" is something of a throw-back to Dick Dudgeon, of the *Devil's Disciple;* that is to say, he is reckless and an outcast, who retains the primitive virtue of not lying to himself.

The scene of the play is a trial for horse-stealing. Blanco is a nominal—not a real—horse-stealer, that is to say, he has committed the sin which a society of horsemen does not pardon. He has run away with the Sheriff's horse, believing it to be his brother's, and taking it on account of a fraudulent settlement of the family estate. A man of his hands, he has yet allowed himself to be tamely captured and brought before a jury of lynchers. Why? Well, he has been upset, overtaken, his plan of life twisted and involved out of all recognition. On his way with the horse, a woman met him with a child dying of croup. She stopped him, thrust the sick child on to the horse, and "commandeered" it for a ride to the nearest doctor's. The child has thrust its weak arms round his neck, and with that touch all the strength has gone out of him. He gives up the horse and flies away into the night, covering his retreat from this new superior force with obscene curses, and surrendering, dismounting, dazed, and helpless, to the Sheriff when the *posse comitatus* catches him.

Thenceforward two opposing forces rend him, and make life unintelligible and unendurable while they struggle for his soul. Dragged into the Sheriff's court, he is prepared to fight for his neck with the rascals who sit in judgment on him, to lie against them, and to browbeat them. Unjust and filthy as they are, he will be unjust and filthy too. But then there was this apparition of the child. What did it mean? Why has it unmanned him? And here it seems to him that God has at once destroyed and tricked him, for the child is dead, and yet his life is forfeit to these brutes. The situation—this sketch of a sudden, ruthless, unintelligible interference with the lives of men—though apparently unknown to the Censor, will be familiar to readers of the Bible and of religious poetry and prose, and Mr. Shaw's treatment of it could only offend either the non-religious mind or the sincerely, but conventionally, pious man who is so wrapt up in the emotional view of religion that its sterner and deeper moralities escape him. The literary parallels will at once occur. Browning chooses the subject in *Pippa Passes*, and in the poem in which he describes how the strong man who had hemmed in and surrounded his enemy suddenly found himself stayed by the "arm that came across" and saved the wretch from vengeance. Ibsen dwells on this divine thwarting and staying power in *Peer Gynt*, and it is, of course, the opening theme of the *Pilgrim's Progress*. As it presents itself to a coarse and reckless, but sincere, man he deals with it in coarse but sincere language—the language which the Censor refuses to pass. Here is the offending passage, which occurs in a dialogue between Blanco and his drunken hypocrite of a brother:—

"BLANCO: Take care, Boozy. He has n't finished

with you yet. He always has a trick up his sleeve.

"ELDER DANIELS: Oh, is that the way to speak of the Ruler of the Universe—the great and almighty God?

"BLANCO: He 's a sly one. He 's a mean one. He lies low for you. He plays cat and mouse with you. He lets you run loose until you think you 're shut of Him; and then when you least expect it, He 's got you.

"ELDER DANIELS: Speak more respectful, Blanco—more reverent.

" BLANCO: Reverent! Who taught you your reverent cant? Not your Bible. It says, 'He cometh like a thief in the night'—aye, like a thief—a horse-thief. And it's true. That 's how He caught me and put my neck into the halter. To spite me because I had no use for Him—because I lived my own life in my own way, and would have no truck with His 'Don't do this,' and 'You must n't do that,' and 'You 'll go to hell if you do the other.' I gave Him the go-bye, and did without Him all these years. But He caught me out at last. The laugh is with Him as far as hanging goes."

Now, let us first note the incapacity of the critic of such an outburst as this to think in terms of the dramatic art—to divine the *état d'âme* of the speaker, and to recognise the method, and, within bounds, the idiosyncracy of the playwright. But having regard to all that the Censor has done and all that he has left undone, let us also mark his resolve to treat as mere blasphemy on Mr. Shaw's part the artist's endeavour to depict a rough man's first consciousness of a Power that, selecting Blanco as it selected Paul and John Bunyan, threatens to drag him through moral shame and physical death, if need be, to life, and not to let him go till He has wrought His uttermost purpose on him. Mr. Shaw naturally makes Blanco talk as an American horse-stealer would talk. But how does Job talk of God, or the Psalmist, or the Author of the Parables? Nearly every one of Blanco Posnet's railings can be paralleled from Job. Listen to this:—

"The tabernacles of robbers prosper, and they that provoke God are secure, into whose hand God bringeth abundantly.

"He removeth away the speech of the trusty, and taketh away the understanding of the aged.

"He taketh the heart of the chief of the people of the earth and causeth them to wander in a wilderness where there is no way.

"They grope in the dark without light, and He maketh them to stagger like a drunken man.

. . . .

"Know now that God hath overthrown me, and hath compassed me with His net.

"He hath fenced up my way that I cannot pass, and He hath set darkness in my paths.

"He hath destroyed me on every side, and I am gone: and mine hope hath He removed like a tree."

Is this blasphemy? Is not Mr. Shaw's theme and its expression a reflection of Job's, save that in the one case a bad man speaks, and in the other a good one? If the answer is that these subjects, these moral and religious relationships, must not be treated on the stage, then we reply first that the Censor is grossly inconsistent, for he did not veto the entire play, but only that passage which most clearly revealed its meaning; secondly, that the licensing of *Everyman*, and of Mr. Jerome's *The Third Floor Back*, where God appears, not merely as an influence on the lives of men, but as a man, sitting at their table and sharing their talk, forbids such an hypothesis; and thirdly, that if Mr. Redford holds this view, he is convicted of opening the drama to horrible mockery of life and sensual trifling with it, and closing it to those close questionings of its purpose, which constitute the main theme of all serious playwrights from Æschylus to Ibsen. That Mr. Shaw could have consented to the omission of the passage we have quoted was out of the question. It is vital. The entire play turns on it. For when the woman comes into court and tells her story, it is seen that the leaven which works in Blanco's mind has leavened the lump; that the prostitute who is for swearing away his life cannot speak, that the ferocious jury will not convict, and the unjust judge will not sentence.

Mr. Shaw had, therefore, to fight for his play, and the Censor has to come into the open and face the music; to reveal his theory of the British drama, and illustrate his continual practice of it; which is to warn off the artist and the preacher, and to clear the path for the scoffer and the clown.

LETTER FROM W. G. BERNARD SHAW TO LADY GREGORY AFTER THE PRODUCTION OF "BLANCO POSNET"

Dear Lady Gregory:

Now that the production of *Blanco Posnet* has revealed the character of the play to the public, it may be as well to clear up some of the points raised by the action of the Castle in the matter.

By the Castle, I do not mean the Lord Lieutenant. He was in Scotland when the trouble began. Nor do I mean the higher officials and law advisers. I conclude that they also were either in Scotland, or preoccupied by the Horse Show, or taking their August holiday in some form. As a matter of fact the friction ceased when the Lord Lieutenant returned. But in the meantime the deputies left to attend to the business of the Castle found themselves confronted with a matter which required tactful handling and careful going. They did their best; but they broke down rather badly in point of law, in point of diplomatic etiquette, and in point of common knowledge.

First, they committed the indiscretion of practically conspiring with an English official who has no jurisdiction in Ireland in an attempt to intimidate an Irish theatre.

Second, they assumed that this official acts as the agent of the King, whereas, as Sir Harry Poland established in a recent public controversy on the subject, his powers are given him absolutely by Act of Parliament (1843). If the King were to write a play, this official could forbid its performance, and probably would if it were a serious play and were submitted without the author's name, or with mine.

Third, they assumed that the Lord Lieutenant is the servant of the King. He is nothing of the sort. He is the Viceroy: that is, he *is* the King in the absence of Edward VII. To suggest that he is bound to adopt the views of a St. James's Palace official as to what is proper to be performed in an Irish theatre is as gross a solecism as it would be to inform the King that he must not visit Marienbad because some Castle official does not consider Austria a sufficiently Protestant country to be a fit residence for an English monarch.

Fourth, they referred to the Select Committee which is now investigating the Censorship in London whilst neglecting to inform themselves of its purpose. The Committee was appointed because the operation of the Censorship had become so scandalous that the Government could not resist the demand for an inquiry. At its very first sitting it had to turn the public and press out of the room and close its doors to discuss the story of a play licensed by the official who barred *Blanco Posnet;* and after this experience it actually ruled out all particulars of licensed plays as unfit for public discussion. With the significant exception of Mr. George Edwards, no witness yet examined, even among those who have most strongly supported the Censorship as an institution, has defended the way in which it is now exercised. The case which brought the whole matter to a head was the barring of this very play of mine, *The Shewing up of Blanco Posnet.* All this is common knowledge. Yet the Castle, assuming that I, and not the Censorship, am the defendant in the trial now proceeding in London, treated me, until the Lord Lieutenant's return, as if I were a notoriously convicted offender. This, I must say, is not like old times in Ireland. Had I been a Catholic, a Sinn Feiner, a Land Leaguer, a tenant farmer, a labourer, or anything that from the Castle point of view is congenitally wicked and coercible, I should have been prepared for it; but if the Protestant landed gentry, of which I claim to be a perfectly correct member, even to the final grace of absenteeism, is to be treated in this way by the Castle, then English rule must indeed be going to the dogs. Of my position of a representative of literature I am far too modest a man to speak; but it was the business of the Castle to know it and respect it; and the Castle did neither.

Fifth, they reported that my publishers had refused to supply a copy of the play for the use of the Lord Lieutenant, leaving it to be inferred that this was done by my instructions as a deliberate act of discourtesy. Now no doubt my publishers were unable to supply a copy, because, as it happened, the book was not published, and could not be published until the day of the performance without forfeiting my American copyright, which is of considerable value. Private copies only were available; but if the holiday deputies of the Castle think that the Lord Lieutenant found the slightest difficulty in obtaining such copies, I can only pity their total failure to appreciate either his private influence or his public importance.

Sixth, they claimed that Sir Herbert Beerbohm Tree, who highly values good understanding with the Dublin public, had condemned the play. What are the facts? Sir Herbert, being asked by the Select Committee whether he did not think that my play would shock religious feeling, replied point-blank, "No, it would heighten religious feeling." He announced the play for production at his theatre; the Censorship forced him to withdraw it; and the King instantly shewed his opinion of the Censorship by making Sir Herbert a Knight. But it also happened that Sir Herbert, who is a wit, and knows the weight of the Censor's brain to half a scruple, said with a chuckle when he came upon the phrase "immoral relations" in the play, "They won't pass that." And they did not pass it. That the deputy officials should have overlooked Sir Herbert's serious testimony to the religious propriety of the play, and harped on his little jest at the Censor's expense as if it were at my expense, is a fresh proof of the danger of transacting important business at the Castle when all the responsible officials are away bathing.

On one point, however, the Castle followed the established Castle tradition. It interpreted the patent (erroneously) as limiting the theatre to Irish plays. Now the public is at last in possession of the fact that the real protagonist in my play who does not appear in person on the stage at all, is God. In my youth the Castle view was that God is essentially Protestant and English; and as the Castle never changes its views, it is bound to regard the divine protagonist as anti-Irish and consequently outside the terms of the patent. Whether it will succeed in persuading the Lord Lieutenant to withdraw the patent on that ground will probably depend not only on His Excellency's theological views, but on his private opinion of the wisdom with which the Castle behaves in his absence. The Theatre thought the risk worth while taking; and I agreed with them. At all events Miss Horniman will have no difficulty in insuring the patent at an extremely reasonable rate.

In conclusion, may I say that from the moment when the Castle made its first blunder I never had any doubt of the result, and that I kept away from Dublin, in order that our national theatre might have the entire credit of handling and producing a new play without assistance from the author or from any other person trained in the English theatres. Nobody who has not lived, as I have to live, in London, can possibly understand the impression the Irish players made there this year, or appreciate the artistic value of their performances, their spirit, and their methods. It has been suggested that I placed *Blanco Posnet* at their disposal only because it was, as an unlicensed play, the refuse of the English market. As a matter of fact there was no such Hobson's choice in the matter. I offered a licensed play as an alternative, and am all the more indebted to Lady Gregory and Mr. Yeats for not choosing it. Besides, Ireland is really not so negligible from the commercial-theatrical point of view as some of our more despondent patriots seem to suppose. Of the fifteen countries outside Britain in which my plays are performed, my own is by no means the least lucrative; and even if it were, I should not accept its money value as a measure of its importance.

G. BERNARD SHAW.

PARKNASILLA,
27 August, 1909.

APPENDIX III

"THE PLAYBOY IN AMERICA"

(*Note to page 180*)

From "THE GAELIC AMERICAN," Oct. 14, 1911

IRISHMEN WILL STAMP OUT THE "PLAYBOY"

October 14, 1911:—"Resolved—That we, the United Irish-American Societies of New York, make every reasonable effort, through a committee, to induce those responsible for the presentation of *The Playboy* to withdraw it, and failing in this we pledge ourselves as one man to use every means in our power to drive the vile thing from the stage, as we drove *McFadden's Row of Flats* and the abomination produced by the Russell Brothers, and we ask the aid in this work of every decent Irish man and woman, and of the Catholic Church, whose doctrines and devotional practices are held up to scorn and ridicule in Synge's monstrosity."

(*Note to page 202*)

From THE NEW YORK "TIMES"

November 28, 1911:—When Christopher Mahon

said: "I killed my father a week and a half ago for the likes of that," instantly voices began to call from all over the theatre:

"Shame! Shame!"

A potato swept through the air from the gallery and smashed against the wings. Then came a shower of vegetables that rattled against the scenery and made the actors duck their heads and fly behind the stage setting for shelter.

A potato struck Miss Magee, and she, Irish like, drew herself up and glared defiance. Men were rising in the gallery and balcony and crying out to stop the performance. In the orchestra several men stood up and shook their fists.

"Go on with the play," came an order from the stage manager, and the players took their places and began again to speak their lines.

The tumult broke out more violently than before, and more vegetables came sailing through the air and rolled about the stage. Then began the fall of soft cubes that broke as they hit the stage. At first these filled the men and women in the audience and on the stage with fear, for only the disturbers knew what they were.

Soon all knew. They were capsules filled with asafœtida, and their odour was suffocating and most revolting.

One of the theatre employes had run to the street to ask for police protection at the outset of the disturbance, but the response was so slow that the ushers and the doortenders raced up the stairs and threw themselves into a knot of men who were standing and yelling "Shame!"

(*Note to page 205*)

From THE NEW YORK "SUN"

Wednesday, November 29, 1911:—Col. Theodore Roosevelt, who had been entertained at dinner prior to the play by Lady Gregory, the author-producer of many of the Irish plays, and Chief Magistrate McAdoo sat with Lady Gregory in one of the lower tier boxes. Col. Roosevelt was there representing the *Outlook*, for he said that if he had any ideas on the subject of the morals and merits of Synge's play he would write them in Dr. Abbott's paper, and Magistrate McAdoo was there for Mayor Gaynor to stop the play if he saw anything contrary to the public morals in it. Mr. McAdoo said that his task was a light one and Col. Roosevelt did not have to say anything. He just applauded.

. . . .

When Col. Roosevelt appeared on a side aisle escorting Lady Gregory to a seat in the box there was a patter of hand clapping and the Colonel gallantly insisted that Lady Gregory should stand and receive the applause.

"He 's here because he smells a fight," said some one in a whisper that rebounded from the acoustic board overhead and was audible all over the house.

When Magistrate McAdoo arrived somebody asked him if he were serving in an official capacity, to which he replied that the Mayor had asked him to drop in and see the play which had so roused the wrath of reputed Irishmen on the night before. He had orders, McAdoo said, to squash it the minute that he should see or hear anything that might be considered to have tobogganed over the line of discretion. But Mr. McAdoo said that he thought he would understand in a fair spirit, withal, the satire and irony of the play, if there was such, and he did not intend to be a martinet. The players graciously handed him out the prompt book between acts to see for himself that the line about "shifts" which had raised a storm of protest in Dublin as being indelicate had been deleted.

Nothing happened during the playing of the little curtain-raiser, *The Gaol Gate*, Lady Gregory's grim little tragedy of suffering Ireland, except that near the end of the single act in the playlet people in the gallery began a noisy warming up on their coughs and sneezes. Some of the plain-clothes men there began to amble around back of the aisles, and they laid their eyes on one individual with a thick neck who seemed about to pull something out from under his coat. Him they landed just as a quick curtain fell on the act and without ado they ousted him.

The citizen began to protest loudly that he was wedged in his seat and could not stir, but two of the strong arms persuaded him that he might as well unwedge himself before something happened. The little interlude was not sufficiently stirring even to attract the notice of those in the balcony and orchestra below.

. . . .

Everybody believed that the trouble was all past with the second act, but the third and last was the noisiest of the three.

It appeared that, failing to find any single line to which they could take exception, those who had come to protest against what they conceived to be the libelling of the Irish race were ready to take it out in one long spell of hissing.

The cue was given when the drunken Michael James, the inn keeper, came on the stage to unite with a maudlin blessing the lovers, Christopher and Margaret.

As in the second act the seat of disturbance was in the balcony and thither six plain-clothes men were hastened. Three heads were together and one man was beating time with his hand while they took relays in hissing. The plain-clothes men descended and the three were yanked from their seats without benefit of explanation.

"But we 're Englishmen," said one of them, "and we take exception to the line, 'Khaki clad cut-throats,' meaning of course the English constabulary."

"And don't call me an Irishman," said the third, while he adjusted his neck gingerly in the collar that had been tightened by the cop's grip. "I 'm a Jew and I was born in St. Joe, Missoury, and I think this play 's rotten, just on general principles. And if I think so I 've got a right to show it. The law holds that anybody has got as good a right to show displeasure at a play as pleasure and I saw my lawyer before I came here, and——"

. . . .

LETTER FROM MR. JOHN QUINN

To the Editor of a Dublin Newspaper

Dear Sir: Now that the Irish players have been to New York and their work seen and judged, the readers of your paper may be interested in the publication of one or two facts in connection with their visit. For some time before the company came to New York there had been threats of an organised attempt by a small coterie of Irishmen to prevent the performance of Synge's *Playboy*. It was difficult for many people in New York who are interested in the drama and art to take these rumours seriously. The attempt to prevent the New York public from hearing the work of these Irish players of course failed. There was an organised attempt by perhaps a hundred or a hundred and fifty Irishmen on the first night *The Playboy* was given here to prevent the performance by hissing and booing, and by throwing potatoes and other objects at the actors, and red pepper and asafœtida among the audience. The disturbers were ejected from the theatre by the police. All the great metropolitan papers, morning and evening, condemned this organised disturbance. The second night, some six or seven disturbers were put out of the theatre by the police, and that was the end of the long-threatened attempt to break up the performance of these plays. The issue was not between the plays and the players and the disturbers, but between the New York public and the disturbers. This fight over Synge was of vast importance for us as a city. One night settled that question and settled it conclusively.

I have seen in some of the daily and one of the weekly Irish papers a statement to the effect that "*The Playboy* was hooted from the stage. . . after the worst riot ever witnessed in a New York playhouse." The statement that it was "hooted from the stage" is of course utterly false. The greatest disorder occurred during the first act. A few minutes after the curtain fell at the end of the first act it was raised again and the statement was made by a member of the company that the act would be given entirely over again. This announcement was greeted with cheers and applause from the great majority of the audience, who indignantly disapproved the attempt of the disturbers to prevent the performance. The play was not "hooted from the stage."

The attempt to prevent by force the hearing of the play having so signally failed, a committee waited upon the Mayor of New York City the next day and demanded the suppression of the plays. The Mayor requested Chief Judge McAdoo of the Court of Special Sessions to attend the play as his representative and report to him. Judge McAdoo is an Irishman, born in Ireland, and has had a distinguished public career as member of Congress, Assistant Secretary of the Navy, and Police Commissioner of New York City, and he is now Chief Judge of the Court of Special Sessions. Judge McAdoo attended the play and made a report to the Mayor completely rejecting the charges that had been made against the morals and ethics of the play.

Both attempts to prevent the performance of the play, the first by force and the second by appeal to the authorities, having completely failed, the work of distorting in the Irish papers what actually took place then began.

Among other things it has been stated that the Abbey Theatre company was not a success in New York. On the contrary the success of the company has been beyond anything in my personal experience. The verdict of critical and artistic New York in favour of the work of the Irish Theatre has been emphatic. The pick of the intellectual and artistic public crowded the theatre during the weeks of the company's performances here and admired and enjoyed their work. In fact intelligent New Yorkers are yet wondering what was the real cause of the attempt to prevent the hearing of the plays. This is one of the mysteries of this winter in New York. I am proud, as a citizen of New York, that New York's verdict of approval was so swift and decisive, and I am proud of New York's quick recognition of the excellence of the new Irish school of drama and acting. As a man of Irish blood, my chief regret is that organised prejudice and prejudgment should have prevented these players from getting that welcome from a section of their own countrymen that I feel sure they will secure in future years. This prejudice was created and the prejudgment was largely caused by the publication of detached sentences and quotations from the plays, while ignoring the art of the actors and the humour and poetry and imaginative beauty of the plays, beauties which, as Sir Philip Sidney would say, "who knoweth not to be flowers of poetry did never walk into Apollo's garden."

Not only have the New York daily papers devoted columns to the work of this company throughout their stay, giving elaborate reviews of their work and long interviews with Lady Gregory and others, but many magazines have had articles on the subject of the plays and writers and on the Irish dramatic movement generally, among others the *Yale Review*, the *Harvard Monthly*, *Collier's Weekly*, the *Nation* (two notices), the *Dramatic Mirror* (five notices), the *Metropolitan Magazine*, *Munsey's Magazine*, the *Craftsman*, *Life*, *Harper's Weekly* (containing repeated notices), the *Outlook*, the *Bookman*, and others. Lady Gregory has contributed articles to the *Yale Review*, the *World of Today* and the *Delineator*, and has lectured at many places upon the Irish dramatic movement. The universities and colleges have shown the liveliest interest in the movement. The professors have lectured upon the plays and the plays have been studied in the college classes and the students have been advised to read them and see the players.

"THE PLAYBOY" IN PHILADELPHIA

(*Note to page 218*)

From Philadelphia "North American"

January 17, 1912:—Determined to force their dramatic views on the public despite the arrests at Monday night's demonstration, several Irishmen last night vented their disapproval of *The Playboy of the Western World* which had its second production by Irish Players at the Adelphi Theatre.

They started by coughing, and they caused the player-folk to become slightly nervous. They next essayed hissing, and cries of "shame," and finally one of their number rose to his feet in a formal protest.

Plain-clothes men throughout the house quelled the slight disturbance, but at every opportunity another belligerent broke into unruly behaviour.

The disorder approached the dignity of serious rioting in the second and third acts of the piece, and at the last a man from Connemara rose in the body of the house, whipped a speech from his coat pocket, and proceeded to interrupt the players with a harangue against the morality of the play.

His philippics were short-lived. Sixteen cops in plain clothes reached him at the same time, and the red man from Connemara disappeared, while the play was being brought to a close. . . .

Extra precautions were taken by the police to preserve order at last night's performance. The lights in the back of the house were not turned down at any time except the first few minutes of the one-act play *Kathleen ni Houlihan* which was the curtain-raiser to the longer piece.

Evidence that there would be trouble later in the evening was plain. Nearly the whole rear part of the house downstairs was filled with Irishmen.

As the little poetic vision of the author unrolled itself and the enthusiastic and for the most part cultured audience was steeping itself in the lyric beauty of the lines, two whole rows of the auditors were seized with a desire to cough or clear their throats. That caused a momentary lull in the play.

Up in the top gallery a thin but insistent ventriloquist piped, "This is rotten!" Cries of "Hush!" quieted the interrupter.

In the first act of *The Playboy* where the bulk of the disturbance occurred Monday night, no expression of opinion was made. But just as every one was settling down to enjoy the play, confident no more interruptions would occur, the trouble began.

One of the clan downstairs cried out his disapprobation. The lights were turned on full tilt, and policemen in plain clothes sprang up from every quarter of the house. Women left their seats in fear. A misguided youth near the orchestra threw his programme, doubled into a ball, at Miss Magee. He was promptly arrested.

The play was stopped for fully five minutes until all the men who showed signs of making trouble were evicted. A number of them laid low, however, and bobbed up now and again, whenever they wanted to. It kept the cops busy hustling them out of the doors. Superintendent Taylor and Captain of the Detectives Souder were in charge of the evictions and as each man was taken out two detectives were sent with him to City Hall where all were locked in.

The climax came when near the close of the last act the man from Connaught began his oratorical flights, drowning the speeches of the actors on the stage.

All interest then centred upon the little knot of strugglers in the main aisle of the theatre and four more Irishmen were escorted, hatless and without overcoats, to the street.

As the men were arraigned at the City Hall, William A. Gray, counsel for the offenders at Monday night's riot, appeared for them. He said he had been sent by Joseph McLaughlin, a saloon-keeper and vice-president of the A. O. H., and he obtained a copy of the charges, with a view to getting the men out on bail. . . . Mr. Gray said he intended taking the matter before the courts and asking for an injunction to prohibit further productions of the play. He said his backer was Joseph McGarrity, a wholesale liquor dealer, in business at 144 South Third Street, who was one of those ejected from the theatre on Monday night.

Headed by Joseph McLaughlin, a delegation of seven prominent members of the Irish societies of the city waited on Mayor Blankenburg yesterday with a petition asking him to stop the production of John M. Synge's comedy *The Playboy of the Western World* on the ground that it is immoral.

The Mayor heard the comments of the Irishmen, but with great good humour pointed out that inasmuch as he could find nothing objectionable in the play, he could not promise to stop the production.

He informed the delegation that he had previously made inquiries of the mayors of New York, Boston, and Providence, where the play had been shown, and had received answers which plainly indicated it was not necessary to stop the play.

(*Note to page 226*)

From PHILADELPHIA "NORTH AMERICAN"

IRISH PLAYERS APPEAR IN A "COURT COMEDY"; NO DECISION

ANSWER CHARGE OF "IMMORALITY" BROUGHT BY A LIQUOR DEALER—"PLAYBOY" DEFENDED AND ATTACKED BY WITNESSES

January 20, 1912:—Second only in point of order, not in worth, was the unadvertised comedy participated in by the Irish Players yesterday afternoon, at a matinee performance held in Judge Carr's room in the quarter sessions court.

The public flocked to see, and stayed to witness, a most complete vindication of Synge's much discussed satirisation of the Irish character. The actors arrested for appearing in *The Playboy of the Western World* kept, however, in the background, while counsel on both sides engaged in lively tilts with two members of the clergy and the judge and other witnesses, furnishing the crowd with entertainment.

Eleven of the Irish Players who were held in $500 bail each by Magistrate Carey, at a hearing in his office earlier in the day, threw themselves upon the mercy of the quarter sessions court, to obtain a legal decision as to whether their play violated the McNichol act of 1911, which makes it a misdemeanor to present "lascivious, sacrilegious, obscene or indecent plays." The hearing before the court was brought about by a habeas corpus proceeding.

Although no decision was handed down after the argument, the attitude of the court was plainly shown, by the line of questions put to various witnesses. The testimony offered by Director of Public Safety Porter, who was called by the commonwealth, indicated that no fault could be found with the play. Judge Carr reserved decision, and adjourned court until Monday.

The defendants were represented by Charles Biddle, William Redheffer, Jr., Howard H. Yocum, and John Quinn, of New York. Directly back of them, in the courtroom, sat Lady Gregory, Mrs. Henry La Barre Jayne, and W. W. Bradford, the latter representing Liebler & Co., managers of the Irish Players.

SURPRISE FOR PROSECUTOR

William A. Gray represented Joseph McGarrity, the liquor dealer, who has taken principal part in the prosecution of the actors. He was aided at times by Assistant District Attorney Fox on behalf of the commonwealth, although the latter's action in calling Director Porter to give testimony caused Mr. Gray both surprise and embarrassment, inasmuch as Mr. Porter said there was nothing in the piece to offend the most devout and reverent of women. He said he had attended the theatre with his wife and that neither of them was "shocked"; on the contrary, distinctly pleased.

Mr. Gray called Joseph McGarrity to the stand. In all seriousness and sincerity the witness testified that, in his opinion, *The Playboy* was a wicked piece and that he thought he had a perfect right to show his disapproval by protesting. He was questioned by Judge Carr as to the reason why he did not leave the theatre before he was ejected, if he thought the play was bad. He could give no adequate reply.

Mr. Gray then read passages from the book, declaring that it had been expurgated to make it presentable on the American stage. Frederick O'Donovan, one of the company, who takes the part of the Playboy, testified that productions of the play had been made in Dublin, Belfast, Cork, London, Oxford, Cambridge, Harrowgate, Boston, New York, New Haven, and Providence without causing any public disturbance except in New York, and without any criminal prosecution being brought anywhere.

It was pointed out to the court by Mr. Gray that Pennsylvania is the only State having a statute preventing immoral or sacrilegious plays and that this was of so recent a date that neither side could argue that other plays of a much more objectionable nature than this had been permitted without hindrance.

Mr. Biddle and Mr. Quinn then summed up their arguments, in which the court concurred, openly. The New York lawyer paid a tribute to Philadelphia concerning the testimony of Director Porter. He said: "Philadelphia ought to be proud of the manhood displayed by such a witness. He stood before this court and testified that he and his wife had witnessed the performance, and that neither was displeased by any exhibition of immorality.

"I say that any man who takes a lascivious meaning out of any of the lines of the play, or who declares that the piece is in any way improper, must have a depraved and an abnormal mind.

"I am ashamed that such men should come here and insult womanhood with their views. The American people are too good a judge of the Irish race to agree with them."

The court then took the case under advisement, reserving decision, counsel agreeing, under his advice, to allow the company to renew its bail bond of $5000.

(*Note to page 242*)

"THE PLAYBOY" IN CHICAGO

From Chicago "Daily Tribune"

January 30, 1913:—Mayor Harrison last night was directed by an order passed by the city council to prohibit the presentation in Chicago of *The Playboy of the Western World*, a play which has caused riots and organised protests in New York, Philadelphia, and Washington when presented by the Irish Players.

What action the mayor will take he was not prepared to indicate at the conclusion of the council session. It was stated during the debate on the subject that the mayor holds discretionary powers, and with the backing of the council can prevent the play if he chooses. But there is nothing mandatory in the order of the council, which asked the mayor to cooperate with Chief of Police McWeeny.

The Mayor said he would investigate the legal phases

Chicago Ill 6

Feb 5th — 1912

Lady Gregory — — — — — — 'ha 'ha,
Foster mother of the funny play boys

this is to console you

from the dread that may fill your grizzly heart after you have read the contents of this note. your fate is sealed. never again shall you gase on the barren hilltops of Connemaras

your doom is sealed

Irelands make believe friends cannot parade in sheeps clothing under my scrutinising eye I scent them to the lair and then 'oi 'oi 'oi OVER

P.S. You would be safe had you stayed in Ireland's but none too late Irelands 10.000 police could not save you death and also look into the character of the play before he decided upon steps to take.

MCINERNEY LEADS FIGHT

Ald. Michael McInerney led the movement for the council order.

"The play is a studied sarcasm on the Irish race," asserted Mr. McInerney, reading from a typewritten sheet; "it points no moral, and it teaches no lesson."

"Press agent!" shouted some one.

"No, I 'm not the press agent," asserted the alderman. "This play pictures an Irishman a coward, something that never happened, and it attacks the Irishwoman. There are no Irishmen connected with the company in any way."

In reply to a question whether Lady Gregory was Irish, McInerney replied he had not met "the lady," and then added:

"There 's a difference in being from Ireland and being Irish. There are lots of people in Ireland that are n't Irish. If you 're born in a stable, that does n't make you a horse."

Mr. Pringle stopped unanimous passage of the resolution.

"While I am not Irish," he said, "I believe Ald. McInerney knows what he is talking about; but I do not know enough about this subject to vote upon it at this time."

"Like Ald. Pringle," said Ald. Thomson, "I am not sufficiently informed, and I shall ask to be excused from voting."

GERMANS STRONG FOR IRISH

"Since some leading Irish organisations have chosen Germans to lead them," said Ald. Henry Utpatel, "I feel that that fact alone makes them a great race, and I shall vote with Ald. McInerney."

"Would you like to hear from the Poles?" asked Ald. Frank P. Danisch.

"That 's all right," said McInerney, "if this play is presented there will come along a play insulting the Poles or some other race. It is not right for Chicago to let any race be insulted."

The order was then adopted, Ald. Pringle and Thomson voting in the negative.

(*Note to page 246*)

FROM CHICAGO "RECORD-HERALD"

February 1, 1912:—Chicago's City Council erred in passing an order directing the mayor and the chief of police to stop the production *The Playboy of the Western World* according to an opinion sent to Mayor Harrison yesterday by William H. Sexton, the city's corporation counsel.

The brief was prepared by William Dillon, brother of John Dillon, the Irish nationalist leader, one of Mr. Sexton's assistants. It held that the counsel order was of no legal effect, although the mayor could suppress the play if he decided that it was immoral or against public policy. Mr. Dillon further declared that the mayor would not be legally right in prohibiting the production.

"I read three pages of the book," declared Mayor Harrison, "and instead of finding anything immoral I found that the whole thing was wonderfully stupid. I shall abide by the corporation's opinion."

Interview for NEW YORK "EVENING SUN"

GEORGE BERNARD SHAW ON THE IRISH PLAYERS

"I presume, Mr. Shaw, you have heard the latest news of your *Blanco Posnet* in America with the Irish Players?" he was asked.

"No. Why? Has it failed?" Mr. Shaw answered.

"Quite the contrary," he was assured.

"Oh, in that case why should I hear about it?" he said. "Success is the usual thing with my plays; it is what I write them for. I only hear about them when something goes wrong."

"But are you not interested in the success of the Irish Players? Or was that a matter of course too?"

"By no means," Mr. Shaw answered. "I warned Lady Gregory that America was an extremely dangerous country to take a real Irish company to."

"But why? Surely America, with its immense Irish element——"

"Rubbish! There are not half a dozen real Irishmen in America outside that company of actors!" he exclaimed. "You don't suppose that all these Murphys and Doolans and Donovans and Farrells and Caseys and O'Connells who call themselves by romantic names like the Clan-na-Gael and the like are Irishmen! You know the sort of people I mean. They call Ireland the Old Country. . . .

"Shall I tell you what they did in Dublin to the Irish Players? There was a very great Irish dramatic poet, who died young, named John Synge—a real Irish name—just the sort of name the Clan-na-Gael never think of.

"Well, John Synge wrote a wonderful play called *The Playboy of the Western World*, which is now a classic. This play was not about an Irish peculiarity, but about a universal weakness of mankind: the habit of admiring bold scoundrels. Most of the heroes of history are bold scoundrels, you will notice. English and American boys read stories about Charles Peace, the burglar, and Ned Kelly, the highwayman, and even about Teddy Roosevelt, the rough-rider. The Playboy is a young man who brags of having killed his father, and is made almost as great a hero as if he were an Italian general who had killed several thousand other people's fathers. Synge satirises this like another Swift, but with a joyousness and a wild wealth of poetic imagery that Swift never achieved. Well, sir, if you please, this silly Dublin Clan-na-Gael, or whatever it called itself, suddenly struck out the brilliant idea that to satirise the follies of humanity is to insult the Irish nation, because the Irish nation is, in fact, the human race and has no follies, and stands there pure and beautiful and saintly to be eternally oppressed by England and collected for by the Clan. There were just enough of them to fill the Abbey Street Theatre for a night or two to the exclusion of the real Irish people, who simply get sick when they hear this sort of balderdash talked about

Ireland. Instead of listening to a great play by a great Irishman they bawled and whistled and sang 'God Save Ireland' (not without reason, by the way), and prevented themselves from hearing a word of the performance. . . ."

"Do you think there will be trouble with the Clan in New York?"

"I think there may be trouble anywhere where there are men who have lost touch with Ireland and still keep up the old bragging and posing. You must bear in mind that Ireland is now in full reaction against them. The stage Irishman of the nineteenth century, generous, drunken, thriftless, with a joke always on his lips and a sentimental tear always in his eye, was highly successful as a borrower of money from Englishmen—both in Old and New England—who indulged and despised him because he flattered their sense of superiority. But the real Irishman of to-day is so ashamed of him and so deeply repentant for having ever stooped to countenance and ape him in the darkest days of the Captivity that the Irish Players have been unable to find a single play by a young writer in which Ireland is not lashed for its follies. We no longer brazen out the shame of our subjection by idle boasting. Even in Dublin, that city of tedious and silly derision where men can do nothing but sneer, they no longer sneer at other nations. In a modern Irish play the hero does n't sing that 'Ould Ireland' is his country and his name it is Molloy; he pours forth all his bitterness on it like the prophets of old.

"The last time I saw an Irish play in Dublin, the

line on which the hero made his most effective exit was 'I hate Ireland.' Even in the plays of Lady Gregory, penetrated as they are by that intense love of Ireland which is unintelligible to the many drunken blackguards with Irish names who make their nationality an excuse for their vices and their worthlessness, there is no flattery of the Irish; she writes about the Irish as Molière wrote about the French, having a talent curiously like Molière.

"In the plays of Mr. Yeats you will find many Irish heroes, but nothing like 'the broth of a boy.' Now you can imagine the effect of all this on the American pseudo-Irish, who are still exploiting the old stage Ireland for all it is worth, and defiantly singing: 'Who fears to speak of '98?' under the very nose of the police—that is, the New York police, who are mostly Fenians. Their notion of patriotism is to listen jealously for the slightest hint that Ireland is not the home of every virtue and the martyr of every oppression, and thereupon to brawl and bully or to whine and protest, according to their popularity with the bystanders. When these people hear a little real Irish sentiment from the Irish Players they will not know where they are; they will think that the tour of the Irish company is an Orange conspiracy financed by Mr. Balfour."

"Have you seen what the Central Council of the Irish County Association of Greater Boston says about the Irish Players?"

"Yes; but please do not say I said so; it would make them insufferably conceited to know that their little literary effort had been read right through by me. You will observe that they begin by saying that they know their Ireland as children know their mother. Not a very happy bit of rhetoric that, because children never do know their mothers; they may idolise them or fear them, as the case may be, but they don't know them.

"But can you conceive a body of Englishmen or Frenchmen or Germans publishing such silly stuff about themselves or their country? If they said such a thing in Ireland they would be laughed out of the country. They declare that they are either Irish peasants or the sons of Irish peasants. What on earth does the son of an American emigrant know about Ireland? Fancy the emigrant himself, the man who has left Ireland to stew in its own juice, talking about feeling toward Ireland as children feel toward their mother. Of course a good many children do leave their mothers to starve; but I doubt if that was what they meant. No doubt they are peasants—a name, by the way, which they did not pick up in Ireland, where it is unknown—for they feel toward literature and art exactly as peasants do in all countries; that is, they regard them as departments of vice—of what policemen call gayety. . . .

"Good heavens!" exclaimed Bernard Shaw, waving a cutting from the *Post* in his hand, "see how they trot out all the old rubbish. 'Noble and impulsive,' 'generous, harum-scarum, lovable characters,' 'generosity, wit, and triumphant true love'; these are the national characteristics they modestly claim as Irishmen who know Ireland as children know their mother. . . ."

"May I ask one more question, Mr. Shaw? Who is the greatest living Irishman?"

"Well, there are such a lot of them. Mr. Yeats could give you off-hand the names of six men, not including himself or myself, who may possibly turn out to be the greatest of us all; for Ireland since she purified her soul from the Clan-na-Gael nonsense, is producing serious men; not merely Irishmen, you understand—for an Irishman is only a parochial man after all—but men in the fullest international as well as national sense—the wide human sense."

"There is an impression in America, Mr. Shaw, that you regard yourself as the greatest man that ever lived."

"I dare say. I sometimes think so myself when the others are doing something exceptionally foolish. But I am only one of the first attempts of the new Ireland. She will do better—probably has done better already—though the product is not yet grown up enough to be interviewed. Good morning."

From "THE GAELIC AMERICAN"

WHAT THE IRISH COUNTY ASSOCIATIONS OF BOSTON SAID OF BERNARD SHAW

January 13, 1912:—The writer of such fool conceptions is as blind as an eight-hour-old puppy to the operation of all spiritual agencies in the life of man. Shaw's writings bear about the same relation to genuine literature as Bryan O'Lynn's extemporised timepiece, a scooped out turnip with a cricket within, does to the Greenwich Observatory. . . .

Shaw stumbles along the bogs, morasses, and sand dunes of literature, without a terminal, leading the benighted and lost wayfarers still farther astray. His unhappy possession of infinite egotism and his utter lack of common sense make of him a *rara avis* indeed, a cross between a peacock and a gander. . . .

In conclusion let us say before we again notice this Barnum of literature he must produce a clean bill of sanity, superscribed by some reputable alienist.

APPENDIX IV

IN THE EYES OF OUR ENEMIES

From "AMERICA"

THE PLAYS OF THE "IRISH" PLAYERS

November 4, 1911:—The editors, like the patriots of the Boyle O'Reilly Club who fêted him in Boston, took Mr. Yeats at his own none too modest estimation. The United Irish Societies of this city denounced *The Playboy*, and an advanced Gaelic organ exposed its barbarities, but gave a clean bill of health to Mr. Yeats and the rest of his programme. Doubtless they also had not read the plays they approved. Well, we have read them. We found several among them more vile, more false, and far more dangerous than *The Playboy*, the 'bestial depravity' of which carries its own condemnation; and we deliberately pronounce them the most malignant travesty of Irish character and of all that is sacred in Catholic life that has come out of Ireland. The details, which are even more shocking than those of *The Playboy*, are too indecent for citation, but the persistent mendacity of the Yeats press agency's clever conspiracy of puff makes it needful to give our readers some notion of their character.

Of Synge's plays only *Riders to the Sea*, an un-Irish adaptation to Connacht fishermen of Loti's *Pecheurs d'Islande*, is fit for a decent audience. None but the most rabidly anti-Catholic, priest-hating bigots could enjoy *The Tinkers' Wedding.*[1] The plot, which involves an Irish priest in companionship with the most degraded pagans and hinges on his love of gain, may not be even outlined by a self-respecting pen. The open lewdness and foul suggestiveness of the language is so revolting, the picture of the Irish priesthood, drawn by this parson's son, is so vile and insulting, and the mockery of the Mass and sacraments so blasphemous, that it is unthinkable how any man of healthy mind could father it or expect an audience to welcome it. This is the "typical Irish play" which the "Irish Players" have presented to a Boston audience.

. . . .

The twain are kindred spirits; but in vileness of caricature and bitterness of anti-Catholic animus, even Synge must yield to Yeats. He also goes to tinkers for his types; and whereas Synge is content with three, and one priest, Yeats's *Where there is Nothing*[1] glorifies a bevy of unbelieving tinkers and presents in contrast a dozen vulgar-spoken monks, who utter snatches of Latin in peasant brogue, while dancing frantically around the altar of God!

[1] Neither *The Tinkers' Wedding* nor *Where there is Nothing* has ever been given by our Company.—A. G.

From "THE GAELIC AMERICAN"

YEATS'S ANTI-IRISH CAMPAIGN

November 18, 1911:—The anti-Irish players come to New York on Nov. 20th, and will appear first in some of the other plays. *The Playboy*, it is announced, will be given later, but the date has not yet been given out. The presentation of the monstrosity is a challenge to the Irish people of New York which will be taken up. There will be no parleying with theatre managers, or appeals to Lady Gregory's sense of decency. *The Playboy* must be squelched, as the stage Irishman was squelched, and a lesson taught to Mr. Yeats and his fellow-agents of England that they will remember while they live.

. . . .

When a woman chooses to put herself in the company of male blackguards she has no right to appeal for respect for her sex.

MRS. MARY F. MCWHORTER, NATIONAL CHAIRMAN, L. A., A. O. H., IRISH HISTORY COMMITTEE, WRITING IN "THE NATIONAL HIBERNIAN," 1913

When it was announced about two months ago that the Abbey players would appear in repertory at the Fine Arts Theatre, in the city of Chicago, I made up my mind to witness all of the Abbey output, if possible, and see if they were as black as some painted them, and now I feel I have earned the right to qualify as a critic.

Having seen them all, I have this to say, that, with

one or two exceptions, they are the sloppiest, and in most cases the vilest, and the most character-assassinating things, in the shape of plays it has ever been my misfortune to see. If, as has been often stated, the plays were written with the intention of belittling the Irish race and the ideals and traditions of that race, the playwrights have succeeded as far as they intended, for the majority of the plays leave us nothing to our credit.

Thinking the matter over now, I cannot understand why *The Playboy* was picked out as the one most dangerous to our ideals. True, *The Playboy* is bad and very bad, but it is so glaringly so, it defeats its own ends by causing a revulsion of feeling.

There are other plays in the collection, however, that are apparently harmless; comedies that will cause you to laugh heartily, 't is true, but in the middle of the laugh you stop as if some one slapped you in the face. You begin to see, in place of the harmless joke, an insidious dig at something you hold sacred, or, if it is something you think is inspiring and patriotic, right in the midst of the thing that carries you away for a few moments on the wings of your lofty dreams and inspirations some monster of mockery will intrude his ugly face, and again the doubt, "Is it ridicule?" The certainty follows the doubt quickly, and you know it is ridicule, and immediately you are possessed of an insane desire to seek out Lady Gregory or some one else connected with the plays and then and there commit murder. That is, you will, if you have the welfare of your race at heart. Of course, if you are careless, or in some cases ignorant of the history of Ireland, or unfamiliar with the conditions there, you will accept the teaching of the Abbey school, and say to yourself, "The Irish are a lazy, crafty, miserly, insincere, irreligious lot after all."

In *The Rising of the Moon* our patriotism is attacked, not openly, of course, but by innuendo. We are made to appear everything but what we are. The policy of "Let well enough alone," is the keynote of this play, bringing out the avarice and selfishness that, according to the Abbey school, is a part of our nature.

It has often been said by our enemies that to have a priest in the family is to be considered very respectable by the average Irish Catholic family, and to bring about this desired result we are willing to sell our immortal souls. All this, not from motives of piety, but to be considered respectable.

In the play *Maurice Harte* this is brought out very forcibly. The family sacrifices everything to keep the candidate for the priesthood in college. The candidate has no vocation, but he is not consulted at all. When this poor, spineless creature sees the members of the family have set their hearts upon his becoming a priest he lets matters drift till the day set for his ordination, and then we behold him going mad. All very far-fetched.

We do admit that we like to have a priest in the family—what Irish mother but will cherish this hope in her bosom for at least one of her sons, or that one of the daughters of the house will become the spouse of Christ? Not, however, from such an unworthy motive as to be considered respectable, but from the pure motive of serving Almighty God.

The Workhouse Ward gives you nothing more edifying than the picture of two hateful old men snarling at each other in a truly disgusting manner.

Coats gives the picture of two seedy, down-at-elbows editors, who, while apparently the best of friends, still are thinking unutterable things of each other.

The Building Fund is a disgusting display of avarice and insincerity. It strikes at the roots of all we hold sacred, and instead of being sincere, religious Catholics, the family is depicted as grasping, miserly creatures, who have no real love for the Church. There is not a redeeming feature in the whole play.

Family Failing, to my notion, is the worst of the output. *Family Failing*, of course, is idleness and all it carries with it. It is a strong witness in favor of that old fallacy, so often repeated by our enemies, that it was not the cruelty of English laws that sent us forth wanderers, but our lazy, idle, shiftless ways. The curtain goes down after the last act of this play on a disgusting spectacle of a lazy uncle snoring asleep on one side of the stage, and his lazy nephew occupying the other side, snoring also.

Kathleen ni Houlihan is beautiful, but every one knows Yeats wrote this before he became a pagan and went astray. His *Countess Cathleen*, written since then, is a weird thing.[1] One can see he strives

[1] The first performance of *The Countess Cathleen* was in 1899; *Kathleen ni Houlihan* was written in 1902.

after his early ideals, but it is a failure, for who can picture a sincere, devout Catholic lady calmly selling her soul to the devil, even though it is to purchase the souls of her poor dependents. And it is a rather dangerous lesson it teaches to the weak minded, when the angel comes to console the weeping peasantry after the countess dies. Supposedly in damnation, he tells them she is saved, because of the good intention she had in selling her soul to Old Nick.

The Magnanimous Lover presents the nasty problem play. Of course our humiliation would not be complete without the "problem play." And the words that this play puts in the mouth of the Irish peasant girl!

My blood boiled as I listened. What on earth do our Irish peasants know about the nasty problems so much affected by certain writers of to-day? American newspaper correspondents have commented from time to time on the chastity of the Irish peasants, and even the hostile ones have marvelled at the complete absence of immorality among them. But what is that to the Irish National (?) dramatists?

It is plain to be seen the self-styled Irish writers affect the present-day style in vogue among French writers. We have seen the result of all this as far as France is concerned. To-day that once proud nation is in a pitiable condition. And so the Abbey crowd would bring about the same undesirable conditions in Ireland if they could. By clever innuendo they would take all the splendid ideals and noble traditions away from the Irish and leave them with nothing high or holy to cling to. But the Abbey butchers will not succeed. They are reckoning without their host. The Irish character is too strong and too noble to be slain by such unworthy methods.

The plays taken as a whole have no literary merit. The backers of the plays preach about Art with a capital A, but they have no artistic merit, for art is truth, and the plays are not true. The great majority of the plays are made up of nothing more than a lot of "handy gab." You can hear the same any day, in any large city in Ireland, indulged in by a lot of "pot boys," or "corner boys," as they are sometimes called. (May I be permitted to use the American vulgarism, "can-rusher," to illustrate what is meant by "corner boy?") Nor is the conversation much more edifying than would be indulged in by those doubtful denizens. . . .

With this dangerous enemy striking at the very strands of our life and from such a dangerous source, the necessity is greater than ever for the men and women of our beloved society to be earnest and honest in their efforts for the revival of Irish ideals. Brothers and Sisters everywhere, place a little history of Ireland in the hand of each little boy and little girl of the ancient race, and all the Lady Gregories in the world will not be able to destroy an atom of our splendid heritage.

APPENDIX V

From "THE OUTLOOK," December 16, 1911

IN THE EYES OF OUR FRIENDS

THE IRISH THEATRE

BY THEODORE ROOSEVELT

In the Abbey Theatre Lady Gregory and those associated with her—and Americans should feel proud of the fact that an American was one of the first to give her encouragement and aid—have not only made an extraordinary contribution to the sum of Irish literary and artistic achievement, but have done more for the drama than has been accomplished in any other nation of recent years. England, Australia South Africa, Hungary, and Germany are all now seeking to profit by this unique achievement. The Abbey Theatre is one of the healthiest signs of the revival of the ancient Irish spirit which has been so marked a feature of the world's progress during the present generation; and, like every healthy movement of the kind, it has been thoroughly national and has developed on its own lines, refusing merely to copy what has been outworn. It is especially noteworthy, and is a proof of the general Irish awakening, that this vigorous expression of Irish life, so honourable to the Irish people, should represent the combined work of so many different persons, and not that of only one person, whose activity might be merely sporadic and fortuitous. Incidentally Lady Gregory teaches a lesson to us Americans, if we only have the wit to learn it. The Irish plays are of such importance because they spring from the soil and deal with Irish things, the familiar home things which the writers really knew. They are not English or French; they are Irish. In exactly the same way, any work of the kind done here, which is really worth doing, will be done by Americans who deal with the American life with which they are familiar; and the American who works abroad as a make-believe Englishman or Frenchman or German—or Irishman—will never add to the sum of first-class achievement. This will not lessen the broad human element in the work; it will increase it. These Irish plays appeal now to all mankind as they would never appeal if they had attempted to be flaccidly "cosmopolitan"; they are vital and human, and therefore appeal to all humanity, just because those who wrote them wrote from the heart about their own people and their own feelings, their own good and bad traits, their own vital national interests and traditions and history. Tolstoy wrote for mankind; but he wrote as a Russian about Russians, and if he had not done so he would have accomplished nothing. Our American writers, artists, dramatists, must all learn the same lesson until it becomes instinctive with them, and with the American public. The right feeling can be manifested in big things as well as in little, and it must become part of our inmost National life before we can add materially to the sum of world achievement. When that day comes, we shall understand why a huge ornate Italian villa or French château or make-believe castle, or, in short, any mere inappropriate copy of some building somewhere else, is a ridiculous feature in an American landscape, whereas many American farm-houses, and some American big houses, fit into the landscape and add to it; we shall use statues of such a typical American beast as the bison—which peculiarly lends itself to the purpose—to flank the approach to a building like the New York Library, instead of placing there, in the worst possible taste, a couple of lions which suggest a caricature of Trafalgar Square; we shall understand what a great artist like Saint-Gaudens did for our coinage, and why he gave to the head of the American Liberty the noble and decorative eagle plume head-dress of an American horse-Indian, instead of adopting, in servile style, the conventional and utterly inappropriate Phrygian cap.

Mary Boyle O'Reilly in the Boston "Sunday Post"

October 8, 1911;—In two shorts weeks the Irish Players have done great and lasting service to every lover of Synge's Irish in Boston; a service long to be held in grateful memory, a creative force of other good to come. Very gravely and conscientiously, Lady Gregory and Mr. William Butler Yeats have trained their players to interpret to the children of Irish emigrants the brave and beautiful and touching memories which, through the ignorance of the second generation, have ceased to be cause for gratitude or pride.

Not this alone: by their fine art, the players have dealt a death blow to the coarse and stupid burlesque of the traditional stage Irishman, who has, for years, outraged every man and woman of Celtic ancestry by gorilla-like buffoonery and grotesque attempts at brogue.

. . . Boston owes Lady Gregory and Mr. Yeats and their company not only grateful thanks, but a very humble apology.

From "The Freeman's Journal"

October 26, 1912:—It is time the Dublin public pulled itself together and began to take a pride in its National Theatre, this theatre which has produced in a few years more than a hundred plays and a company of players recognised as true artists, not only by their fellow-countrymen, but by the critics of England and America. The Abbey Theatre has made it possible for a writer living in Ireland and writing on Irish subjects to win a position of equal dignity with his fellow-artist in London or Paris; it has made it possible for an Irish man or woman with acting ability to play in the plays of their fellow-countrymen, and to earn a decent living and win a position of equal respect with any English or Continental actor.

From New York "Journal"

December 18, 1911:—The hysterics and rowdyism that attended the opening of the Irish plays in New York having died away, listen to a few facts concerning the extremely interesting and valuable work of Lady Gregory and her associates, the Irish playwrights and actors.

Some of those entirely ignorant of that which they discussed thought that the Irish players were wilfully irreligious, and others equally ignorant thought that they were weakly lacking in Irish patriotism.

As a matter of fact, the Irish playwrights and actors . . . are thoroughly imbued with the Irish spirit and are trying as well as they can to present certain Irish conditions and characters as they are, utilising literature and the drama as mediums.

. . . It was thought by some good people who had not seen the plays that they were irreligious in character and showed lack of respect especially for the Catholic faith. But this is not true.

In the play called *Mixed Marriage* all the bigotry and religious stupidity is shown by the old Protestant father. The unselfishness, real patriotism, courage, and broad-minded humanity in this play are the possessions of the Catholics—as is, indeed, usually the case in Ireland.

It is interesting to observe how real merit wins and overcomes ignorant prejudice.

Many of the very men that hissed and hooted at

the Irish plays on the first night without listening to them now attend the performances regularly.

Those that enjoy most thoroughly the wonderful wit and pathos of the Irish race, as shown in these plays, are those Irish men and women.

Sara Allgood, as the old patient wife and mother in *Mixed Marriage*, is a perfect picture of the womanhood that has created Ireland.

Lady Gregory and her friends have rendered a real service to this country and to Ireland by bringing the plays here.

ANONYMOUS IN CHICAGO "DAILY TRIBUNE"
February, 1912

TO LADY GREGORY

Long be it e'er to its last anchorage
Thy oaken keel, O "Fighting Temeraire,"
Shall forth beyond the busy harbour fare.
Still mayest thou the battle royal wage
To show a people to itself; to gauge
The depth and quality peculiar there;
Of its humanity to catch the air
And croon its plaintiveness upon the stage.

Nay, great and simple seer of Erin's seers,
How we rejoice that thou wouldst not remain
Beside thy hearth, bemoaning useless years,
But hear'st with inner ear the rhythmic strain
Of Ireland's mystic overburdened heart
Nor didst refuse to play thy noble part!